PENGUIN BOOKS

SHAKEDOWN

James Bovard is the author of *Lost Rights: The Destruction of American Liberty*, *The Fair Trade Fraud*, and *The Farm Fiasco*. A frequent contributor to *The Wall Street Journal* and *The New York Times*, he has also written for publications that include *The Washington Post*, *Newsweek*, and *The American Spectator*. He lives in Washington, D.C.

SHAKEDOWN

How the Government Screws You from A to Z

James Bovard

PENGUIN BOOKS

PENGUIN BOOKS
Published by the Penguin Group
Penguin Books USA Inc., 375 Hudson Street, New York, New York 10014, U.S.A.
Penguin Books Ltd, 27 Wrights Lane, London W8 5TZ, England
Penguin Books Australia Ltd, Ringwood, Victoria, Australia
Penguin Books Canada Ltd, 10 Alcorn Avenue, Toronto, Ontario, Canada M4V 3B2
Penguin Books (N.Z.) Ltd, 182–190 Wairau Road, Auckland 10, New Zealand

Penguin Books Ltd, Registered Offices: Harmondsworth, Middlesex, England

First published in the United States of America by Viking Penguin,
a division of Penguin Books USA Inc. 1995
Published in Penguin Books 1996

1   3   5   7   9   10   8   6   4   2

THE LIBRARY OF CONGRESS HAS CATALOGUED THE HARDCOVER AS FOLLOWS:
Bovard, James.
Shakedown: how the government screws you
from A to Z/James Bovard.
p.   cm.
ISBN 0-670-86542-7 (hc.)
ISBN 0 14 02.5819 1 (pbk.)
1. Civil rights—United States.   2. Liberty.   3. Government, Resistance to—
United States.   4. Trade regulation—United States.   I. Title.
JC599.U5B599   1995
323.4´9´0973—dc20   95–18515

Printed in the United States of America
Set in Garamond 3
Designed by James Sinclair

Dedicated to the victims of the State

INTRODUCTION

How little important it is to destroy a government, in comparison with destroying the prestige of government.

—*Albert Jay Nock*

A Gallup Poll released in April 1995 revealed that 39 percent of Americans believe that "the federal government has become so large and powerful it poses an immediate threat to the rights and freedoms of ordinary citizens." The poll results sent a sonic boom across the horizon in Washington, D. C., where politicians preach that citizens have a duty to trust their government—and where President Bill Clinton repeatedly denounces public cynicism about the goodness of government. The poll found that roughly equal percentages of liberals, conservatives, and centrists perceive government as a dire threat to their rights and liberties.

The Gallup Poll results should have come as no surprise—considering that government has become far more powerful in recent decades and is crushing the lives and hopes of more and more Americans. Millions of Americans have lost the right to control their own land, to modify their own homes, to own a weapon for self-defense, to raise their own children as they think best, to learn about new medical treatments, and to live peacefully without interference from undercover government agents looking to create a crime.

This book seeks to provide readers with a survey of government abuses. While many Americans may be familiar with the depredations of the IRS, or with outrageous cases of police brutality, or with the storm trooper tactics of the federal Bureau of Alcohol, Tobacco and Firearms, many people do not realize that other federal agencies—such as HUD, the FDA, the EPA—are also guilty of outrages against the citizenry. And local and state governments have also too often plundered their citizens in the name of law enforcement.

The thicker that government statute books become, the greater the imbalance in power between the citizen and the State. Government officials are imposing tens of millions of penalties on private citizens every year, often for "crimes" that were never recognized as offenses or problems until recently. Washington lawyer James DeLong has written eloquently about what he calls the "New Criminalization" from today's Big Government:

> The use of punitive measures to control vast areas of private life and economic activity has exploded. . . . A destructive dynamic is being created by their sheer volume and breadth, by the complexity of the requirements and uncertainties of compliance, by the declining relevance of knowledge or intent, by the propensity to use punitive measures as a first resort rather than last, and by a failure to analyze seriously the moral nature of the conduct that is criminalized. . . .

We need fewer laws. Every unnecessary law undermines the enforcement of necessary laws. Laws are not simply political wish-lists and planks in political reelection campaigns, but acts forcibly administering on people's lives.

We need rigorous enforcement of laws against murder, assault, rape, robbery, fraud, and other "traditional" crimes. It would be far better for government to adequately enforce a few dozen laws than to promulgate thousands of regulations and generally neglect public safety.

In contemporary political thought, there are almost no principles upon which the citizen can resist the State—almost no principle that would decree where the government must cease the expansion of its power, almost no principle on which the individual can stand against the State and rest his claims upon inviolable rights. The entire notion of the citizen's inviolability has been buried beneath a thousand demands for government intervention to achieve a certain preferred end or benefit a certain politically preferred group. Since there are no principles upon which to resist the government, it is not surprising that the government continually expands year by year, encroaching ever further into people's lives.

We owe it to ourselves and to our children to stand up and reclaim the liberty that once made this nation revered around the world. Supreme Court Justice Noah Swayne declared in 1873, "That only is a free government, in the American sense of the term, under which the inalienable right of every citizen to pursue his happiness is unrestrained, except by just, equal, and impartial laws."

SHAKEDOWN

AFFIRMATIVE ACTION:

A Government License
to Pigeonhole

If a business does not adopt racial hiring quotas, federal agencies can seek to financially destroy the business even when there is no proof it ever discriminated against a black or Hispanic job seeker. The Equal Employment Opportunity Commission routinely forces companies to pay handouts to alleged victims of discrimination who never even applied for jobs. Instead of promoting fair treatment, affirmative action is arbitrarily thwarting the lives of millions of people who are not in politically favored racial or ethnic groups.

The EEOC, since its creation in 1964, has devoted itself to subverting federal law and increasing its own power. The original 1964 Civil Rights Act required that an employer must have shown an *intent to discriminate* before being proven guilty. However, by the late 1960s, the EEOC had established a definition of discrimination far wider than Congress authorized. EEOC chairman Clifford Alexander announced in 1968: "We . . . here at EEOC believe in numbers. . . . Our most valid standard is in numbers. . . . The only accomplishment is when we look at all those numbers and see a vast improvement in the picture."

The history of the EEOC exemplifies how government agencies can achieve near-absolute power simply by issuing incomprehensible regulations.

* In late 1991, the EEOC compelled a $2 million settlement out of World's Finest Chocolate, a Chicago candy maker. EEOC's Allison Nichol explained: "Their method of recruitment was primarily by word of mouth through their existing workforce, which at the time was primarily white, thereby excluding blacks from knowing about the jobs."

* The EEOC has sued Hooters restaurants because they refuse to hire male waiters. Hooters hires only female waitresses, and women in semi-scanty jogging suits are the chain's trademark. One former high-ranking EEOC official told me that female lawyers at EEOC are anxious to attack Hooters because they want to bust up a major sexist restaurant-bar chain. But, as one Hooters official observed, "Hooters girls are the essence of the Hooters concept." EEOC officials apparently deny that only women can satisfy the special "bona fide occupational qualifications" required by a restaurant named Hooters.

* Shelby Steele, a black professor at San Jose State University in California, observes, "In the late sixties and early seventies, affirmative action underwent a remarkable escalation of its mission from simple antidiscrimination enforcement to social engineering by means of quotas, goals, timetables, set-asides and other forms of preferential treatment."

* Former White House counsel Boyden Gray and former EEOC chairman Evan Kemp noted in 1993, "Any substantial difference among racial, ethnic or gender groups in the proportions hired or promoted can make an employer the target of a lawsuit charging 'disparate impact.' Yet it is hardly surprising that in many labor markets and firms, such disparate results occur even when employers assiduously avoid group-based discrimination. . . . The Department of Education reported in 1990 that 12 percent of white 20 year olds, 22 percent of African Americans and 40 percent of Hispanics had failed to complete high school.

* Federal agencies have long paved the way for affirmative action mandates. The types of policies imposed upon government per-

sonnel practices have repeatedly paved the way for subsequent government mandates for private hiring. One sign of the future: The Food and Drug Administration put out an "Equal Employment Opportunity Handbook" that provided guidelines for hiring. As Stuart Taylor of *Legal Times* reported, the handbook declared that "the common requirement for 'knowledge of rules of grammar' and 'ability to spell accurately' in clerical and secretarial job descriptions" should be shunned because it may impede courtship of " 'underrepresented groups or individuals with disabilities.' " Nor should interviews be used "to judge highly subjective traits such as motivation, ambition, maturity, personality and neatness." Since federal managers are not allowed to consider literacy, maturity, or neatness in hiring secretaries, the only alternative is to hire by racial quotas.

★ The U.S. Forest Service may have achieved the apex of affirmative action idealism. The Forest Service was harshly criticized in the past for not hiring enough female firefighters. Many women could not pass the strength tests required for lugging heavy firefighting equipment, etc. The agency's solution? Modifying its position announcements. One job announcement declared, "Only unqualified applicants may apply." A second announcement specified, "Only applicants who do not meet [job requirement] standards will be considered." The *Washington Times* noted, "An internal Forest Service document indicates that, in some cases, critical firefighting positions were left vacant or filled with unqualified temporary workers because no women applied for the posts." Republican Representative Wally Herger of California denounced the agency for "quota lunacy" and declared, "It is not a civil right to land a job for which one is unqualified. This is ridiculous."

ASSAULT WEAPONS BAN:

First Step to Seizing Thirty Million Guns

Congress enacted legislation last year that could be the first step to the confiscation of tens of millions of private rifles, shotguns, and pistols. Though the new law purportedly targets only "assault weapons," the loose definitions and expansive goals of the antigun lobby and federal antigun agents could easily lead to a long list of weapons targeted for seizure.

According to the Defense Department, an assault weapon is a rifle that can fire both automatically (like a machine gun) and semiautomatically (a single shot for each trigger squeeze). The federal government has severely restricted the ownership of machine guns since 1934, and legally owned machine guns have had almost no role in violent crime in the last half century. But politicians and most of the news media have a much more expansive concept of "assault weapon." The federal ban targets semiautomatic guns with certain military-type features—but the semiautomatic guns targeted are functionally fundamentally the same as guns that have been sold in the United States for over a hundred years. According to author David Kopel, if all semiautomatic guns were banned, the federal government would confiscate over thirty-five million weapons.

★ Democratic Senator John Rockefeller of West Virginia was a fervent supporter of the crime bill and the assault weapons ban. A few days after the bill had passed the Senate, the *Charleston Daily Mail* reported from Washington, "If burglars are casing big houses around here, they may want to give wide berth to the Rockefeller mansion. The occupant is packing heat and knows how to use it. Sen. Jay Rockefeller disclosed that for the past 25 years he has been the proud owner of a Colt AR-15, a so-called assault weapon used in Vietnam. Rockefeller keeps the rifle in his Washington home." This was news to the Washington police, which bans the ownership of AR-15s in the District of Columbia. After Rockefeller was told that having such a gun in the district was a crime, he "remembered" that he actually kept the gun stored in northern Virginia. Rockefeller also claimed that he was unaware that the District of Columbia banned such guns. Rockefeller has private security guards around his lavish Washington home, and the Senate office buildings where he works are heavily guarded by well-fed Capitol policemen. Yet he still feels entitled to own a gun that he worked to prohibit other Americans from purchasing.

The opponents of the assault weapons ban were ridiculed for their excessive fear of government—for their argument that the federal ban was only the first step to a confiscation of guns. How have assault weapons bans operated on local and state levels?

✴ New York City required rifle owners to register their guns in 1967; city council members at that time promised that the registration lists would not be used for a general confiscation of law-abiding citizens' weapons. Roughly one million New Yorkers were obliged to register with police. The *New York Times* editorialized on September 26, 1967, "No sportsman should object to a city law that makes it mandatory to obtain a license from the Police Department and to register rifles. . . . Carefully drawn local legislation would protect the constitutional rights of owners and buyers. The purpose of registration would be not to prohibit but to control dangerous weapons."

✴ In 1991, Mayor David Dinkins railroaded a bill through the City Council banning possession of many semiautomatic rifles, claiming that they were actually assault weapons. Dinkins claimed that the rifles were a grave safety threat—even though the police records contained almost no cases of the registered guns being used in crimes. Thousands of residents who had registered in 1967 and scrupulously obeyed the law were stripped of their right to own their guns. One NYPD spokesman announced that "spot checks are planned" to ensure that people have complied with the law. Spot checks, aka searches without a warrant.

Jerold Levine, counsel to the New York Rifle Association, observed: "Tens of thousands of New York veterans who kept their rifles from World War II or the Korean war have been turned into felons as a result of this law. Even the puny target shooting guns in Coney Island arcades have been banned under the new law because their magazines hold more than five rounds."

* The crime bill's assault weapons provision is similar to a ban enacted in Columbus, Ohio. A federal appeals court, in a decision completely ignored by the media, nullified Columbus's assault weapons ban as unconstitutional on July 11, 1994. A panel of federal judges declared, "The ordinance purports to ban 'assault weapons,' but, in fact, it bans only an arbitrary and ill-defined subset of these weapons without providing any explanation for its selections." The judges concluded that the law "is fundamentally irrational and impossible to apply consistently by the buying public, the sportsman, the law enforcement officer, the prosecutor or the judge."

* A Supreme Court decision from June 1994 sheds light on how the assault weapons ban will likely be administered. Harold Staples of Oklahoma owned a semiautomatic rifle, an AR-15; the BATF raided his home, found the gun, and confiscated it, claiming that it was actually a machine gun—an automatic weapon. (The National Firearms Act of 1934 bans possession of unregistered, unlicensed machine guns.) The BATF argued in court that the gun had been illegally modified so that it could fire more than one bullet with each trigger pull—the technical definition of an automatic weapon. Staples swore that, when he operated the gun, it fired only one shot per trigger pull, and functioned poorly

at that. Each violation of the National Firearms Act can be pun-
ished by up to ten years in prison. (Stephen Halbrook notes that
the BATF, after it confiscates a person's guns, routinely tampers
with the guns to make them shoot automatically—and then
drags the person into court on trumped-up charges. In a similar
case in 1988, the BATF prosecuted a Pennsylvania policeman,
James Corcoran, for the crime of selling machine guns. As in the
Staples case, the guns were AR-15s. At trial, BATF admitted that
it had tampered with the guns to make them fire more than one
shot when the trigger was pulled. Federal Judge Donald Ziegler
denounced the BATF's action as "a severe miscarriage of justice,"
and a jury rejected all of the federal charges against Corcoran.)

* The Clinton administration asserted that gun owners must be
  presumed guilty even in cases where they had no intention to
  break the law. The Supreme Court, in a 7–2 decision rejecting the
  administration's arguments written by Justice Clarence Thomas,
  declared, "The government's position, is precisely that 'guns in
  general' are dangerous items. [For] the Government . . . the prop-
  osition that a defendant's knowledge that the item he possessed
  'was a gun' is sufficient for a conviction." Justice Thomas pillo-
  ried the Clinton administration's position: "In the Government's
  view, any person . . . who simply has inherited a gun from a rel-
  ative and left it untouched in an attic or basement, can be subject
  to imprisonment, despite absolute ignorance of the gun's firing
  capabilities, if the gun turns out to be an automatic."

* The Clinton administration implicitly argued before the Supreme
  Court that gun owners are the legal equivalent of drug dealers. To
  justify their claim that gun owners must be presumed guilty, government prosecutors cited cases involving the presumption of guilt
  under the federal Narcotics Act of 1914. (At one point in the case,
  federal prosecutors argued that "one would hardly be surprised to
  learn that owning a gun is not an innocent act.") Since drug dealers are automatically assumed to know they are violating federal
  narcotics laws, the Clinton administration claimed that gun owners must be presumed to know when they violate federal gun laws.

ASSET FORFEITURE:

Hundreds of Thousands of
Government Robbery Victims

Did you know that even if you are completely innocent, federal agents can seize your home, your car, and your wallet—and force you to spend thousands of dollars in legal fees trying to get them back?

Under newly devised "asset forfeiture" laws and regulations, thousands of American citizens are being stripped of their property based solely on rumors and unsubstantiated assertions made by government confidential informants.

Federal agents can now seize private property under more than two hundred federal statutes. Since 1984, federal agencies have confiscated over $4 billion in cash and property from American citizens.

The vast majority of people whose property is seized by federal, state, and local officials are never formally charged with a crime.

* In Chicago, police confiscate the car of anyone who is found to be traveling with an unregistered handgun.

* Customs Service agents seized $19,000 from Gilberto and Josefina Gomez, two farm laborers, crossing back into Mexico at the El Paso border crossing in April 1994. The Gomezes offered proof that the $19,000 was money received from a worker's com-

pensation settlement after Gilberto was injured while harvesting vegetables. (He intended to use the money to start a business in Mexico.) The Customs Service did not file any criminal charges against the couple, but still refuses to give the money back. (Customs did offer to give $13,000 back if the Gomezes would agree to let the U.S. government keep the balance, but the Gomezes refused.)

* In Iowa, a woman accused of shoplifting a $25 sweater had her $18,000 car—specially equipped for her handicapped daughter—seized as the "getaway vehicle."

* Police seized over $1,000 in cash when they raided the home of Percy Ormeno, a Daly City, California, T-shirt vendor, to search for drugs. The cops found no drugs—but they did find a piece of paper which they claimed was a record of a drug sale. The evidence was so flimsy that they never even showed it to a local prosecutor. As Gary Webb noted in a 1993 series of articles in the *San Jose Mercury News* on forfeiture abuses, "All it takes to lose your money is an unconvincing or undocumented explanation of where you got it."

* Utah police in 1991 raided the home of Vera and Robert Garcia, an elderly couple in Ogden, Utah, and confiscated their house, retirement savings, and a few hundred dollars cash on the premises. The police claimed that almost everything the Garcias owned was the product of narcotics dealing. Though the police have offered no evidence to justify the seizure, they refuse to return the property.

* In 1994, the U.S. Department of Justice sued TitanSports, the World Wrestling Federation, and wrestling organizer Vincent McMahon, claiming that the organization had been illegally distributing steroids from 1985 to 1991 at its Titan Tower headquarters in Fairfield, Connecticut. Federal prosecutors may have been captivated by their proposed seizure of the hundred-thousand-square-foot, $8 million building. But their paperwork

was not as good as their property lust: TitanSports never occupied the building until after the six years that the feds alleged the building had been used by the company for illicit steroid distribution. After a jury found the accused not guilty on all charges, McMahon, the organizer of the World Wrestling Federation, declared: "Just like in wrestling, the good guys always win."

✳ Federal attorneys seized the home of Walter and Joann Cwikla in East Hartland, Connecticut, in 1989 solely because an anonymous informant allegedly asserted that several years earlier Joann Cwikla allowed someone briefly to store marijuana in the house's garage. Federal agents did not even bother to search the home before they posted a notice on the door declaring that the house had been seized. Five years later, the Cwiklas were still battling federal attorneys in court over the case; the government offered to drop the case if the Cwiklas paid $25,000, but they refused.

✳ In 1994, a federal judge slammed federal prosecutors for confiscating a four-thousand-acre, $6 million ranch in Glades County, Florida. The prosecutors claimed that the owners of the ranch had been involved in drug smuggling. The only evidence that the prosecutors had was the fact that a twin-engine plane crashed nearby on an Indian reservation. The government claimed that the plane was heading for the ranch when it crashed—and thus justified seizing the ranch for the six years that the court case dragged out. (One federal attorney bragged that they had grabbed a multimillion-dollar ranch at the cost to the government of only a few thousand dollars' paperwork.) Toni Wiersma, one of the owners, observed after the verdict: "The shocking thing is the way the seizure laws are, no one is safe, and there are no repercussions if prosecutors make a mistake."

✳ Oyster Bay, Long Island, recently announced a new policy of "zero tolerance for graffiti." Police are now authorized to confiscate any vehicle (bicycle, skateboard, or Honda Accord) used in the commission of a graffiti crime. Town Clerk Carl Marcellino told *Newsday* that the new law is an attempt "to reclaim our town. Graffiti is an international blight on localities." (Marcellino did not offer any evidence to show that the graffiti in Oyster Bay was part of a foreign conspiracy.)

* In March 1991, federal agents raided fraternity houses at the University of Virginia and confiscated a $395,000 frat house after they discovered a few hundreds dollars' worth of marijuana. Local police at a press conference at the time of the seizure compared their conquest of the frat house to the then-recent U.S. victory over Iraq: "We had a deadline, we had an enemy and we had a coalition force. We went in there and did the same thing we had just done to Hussein."

* Police in Oxnard, California, seized an entire city block because of allegations of drug sales by one business tenant on the block. After four years and hundreds of thousands of dollars in legal fees, the police were forced to return most of the property to the innocent owners.

* In November 1994, a federal appeals court in California struck down the seizure of $30,060 from a motorist based on a police dog's bark. Police stopped Albert Alexander for allegedly running a stop sign. The officers who stopped him found a large bag of money on the front seat. The police searched the car but found no drugs. The officers called in their trump card—a police dog who barked when he sniffed the money. This supposedly proved that the money was tainted with drug residue—and thereby proved, to the officers' satisfaction, that the money was illicit profits of narcotics deals. Alexander sued the government to get the money returned. At trial, one forensic toxicologist testified that up to 75 percent of U.S. currency is coated with traces of cocaine. The appeals court concluded, "If greater than 75 percent of all circulated currency in LA is contaminated with drug residue, it is extremely likely a narcotics detection dog will positively alert when presented with a large sum of currency." It took Alexander almost five years and thousands of dollars in legal costs to get his money back.

* In Arizona, the vast majority of the eight hundred cars seized from citizens since 1990 by state and local police were taken from

people never charged with a crime, as the *Arizona Republic* reported. While Arizona had a stringent asset forfeiture law designed to help break the backs of major drug dealers, the average amount of property or cash confiscated by police from citizens was barely $3,000.

✦ Helper, Utah, in January 1995, created a new policy designed to let police officers keep up to 25 percent of any cash or property they seize from *suspected* drug dealers. Helper Mayor Mike Dalpiaz explained the program's rationale: "Why not give our guys a reason to be more aggressive?" The mayor observed, "This doesn't cost the city a thing; it's a wash. If the city gets a house through a drug forfeiture, and we put it on the market and sell it for $50,000, then by God the guy who made the bust is going to get a nice bonus check for his work."

✦ If the citizen wants to get his property back after it was seized by the federal government, he must post a bond equal to 10 percent of the property's value to cover the government's costs in defending itself against his lawsuit. Legal costs for suing the government to recover one's property can easily exceed $10,000. Thus, if the government seizes only a few handfuls of cash or an old car, the citizen cannot possibly break even by suing to recover his property.

Because government officials have vast discretion in how they spend confiscated loot, many police agencies keep all or most of what they seize, often using the money to buy lavish equipment or fancy cars for themselves:

✦ In Greensboro, North Carolina, police used assets seized from private citizens to pay for an equipment-filled exercise room for themselves.

✦ In Erie County, New York, Sheriff Thomas Higgins used money from the forfeiture fund to buy himself a fancy red Ford Crown Victoria—after the county government had refused to allocate money for the car from the county budget.

★ In Suffolk County, New York, the local prosecutor has been widely denounced for driving a lavish new BMW that local police confiscated from drug suspects.

★ In Illinois, local and state police operate on an "honor system" in their use and disposal of confiscated assets from private citizens. Thus, the police give themselves a far greater benefit of the doubt than they allow to the property owners.

★ A report by the Arizona auditor general in 1993 concluded that many state agencies could not account for the property that they had confiscated, and noted that law enforcement might "target suspects based on the value of the suspects' assets . . . before an investigation is begun or charges are filed."

★ In Marin County, California, the county narcotics unit used $227,000 that it had received from the federal government as its share of confiscated property to settle a lawsuit from a police-woman on the local antidrug unit who claimed that two police-men in the unit sexually harassed her. After the controversy over the dubious use of seized money hit the newspapers, U.S. Attorney Michael Yamaguchi in San Francisco defended the asset forfeiture program: "It's a very successful program. It has lots and lots of money."

★ Asset forfeiture also encourages thefts by the police. Twenty-six members of the elite narcotics squad of the Los Angeles County Police were convicted in 1994 for stealing money from drug suspects. Some of them even tried to rationalize their behavior, reasoning that if the government was allowed to steal money, why shouldn't they? County Sheriff Sherman Block said: "I don't know how you can draw an analogy between the asset forfeiture program, which is a matter of law . . . and sticking a hand in and helping yourself to what's available." Unfortunately, since forfeiture laws are so vague and expansive, there may be little or no difference in practice.

CAFE STANDARDS:

Death by Regulation

A federal safety agency has knowingly promulgated regulations that result in the bloody deaths of thousands of Americans in car accidents each year. Yet the agency continues to pretend that it has no responsibility or accountability for its actions.

In 1975, after the panic over the Arab oil embargo, Congress decided to solve the nation's energy problems by forcing car manufacturers to build cars that got better gas mileage.

CAFE—the Corporate Average Fuel Economy regulations—currently require that each automaker's production achieve at least 27.5 miles per gallon on average.

Automakers have achieved compliance with federal fuel economy dictates primarily by sharply reducing the weight of new cars. But, as lawyer Sam Kazman notes, "large cars are generally more crashworthy than small cars, owing to their heavier construction, their greater crush space to absorb collision forces, and their larger occupant space."

Federal CAFE standards, stripped of their verbiage, are simply a government command to build smaller, lighter cars. This is fine for federal agency annual reports bragging about increases in gas mileage. However, for private citizens in auto accidents, CAFE has often been the kiss of death.

A 1989 study by economist Robert Crandall of the Brookings Institute and John Graham of the Harvard School of Public Health concluded that the CAFE standards resulted in auto manufacturers building cars that weighed on average five hundred pounds less than they otherwise would have weighed. The lighter cars resulted in a 14 to 27 percent increase in auto traffic fatalities—an additional 2,200 to 3,900—and up to 20,000 serious injuries over the ten-year lifetime of 1989 model cars.

The *New York Times* noted in an editorial in 1991: "CAFE has meant more fatalities and serious injuries as manufacturers have been forced to sell smaller cars to meet the standards."

* The National Academy of Sciences concluded in a 1992 report, "It may be inevitable that significant increases in fuel economy can occur only with some negative safety consequences."

* The Insurance Institute for Highway Safety reported in 1991 that the occupant death rates in the smallest 1988 model year cars were nearly three times the death rates in the largest cars."

* An American Automobile Association report noted in 1993 that federal "statistics show that small cars account for more serious injuries and about twice as many deaths as large cars."

* The Insurance Institute for Highway Safety reported in 1991, "Downsizing cars means more deaths."

* The Competitive Enterprise Institute (CEI) sued the National Highway Traffic Safety Administration (NHTSA), which administers the CAFE standards. CEI's Sam Kazman accused the agency of "deliberately concealing" the safety issue: "Until they have express authorization to kill people in the name of improving fuel economy, they ought not to be doing that."

* In 1992, a federal appeals court hit the U.S. Transportation Department on the CAFE standards, ruling that the agency had "fudged the analysis," used "statistical legerdemain" and "spe-

cious arguments," "obscured the safety problem," and "cowered behind bureaucratic mumbojumbo," and concluded, "Nothing in the record or in NHTSA's analysis appears to undermine the inference that the 27.5 mpg standard kills people."

The court bluntly declared, "By making it harder for consumers to buy large cars, the 27.5 mpg standard will increase traffic fatalities. . . . When the government regulates in a way that prices many of its citizens out of access to large-car safety, it owes them reasonable candor."

The court remanded the regulations to NHTSA and demanded that the agency examine how its CAFE standard may impact auto safety. The agency effectively shrugged off the court's order, simply announcing that its regulations had no effect on safety. CEI sued the agency to force it to comply with the 1992 court decision. At a hearing on the case, federal judge Douglas Ginsburg observed that the only thing NHTSA employees seemed to care about was being able to leave their office by 5 P.M. each day.

Last February (1995), the federal appeals court ruled that the agency failed to offer any meaningful response to the Harvard-Brookings study showing higher fatalities caused by the CAFE standard. But the judges, ever forgiving to bureaucrats too busy to obey the law, refused to find the agency violated the law.

Confiscation via
Wildlife Accusation

Hundreds of thousands of Americans' lives have been severely disrupted by federal sanctification of species such as *Soccorro isopod,* the Texas wild rice plant, the fringe-toed lizard, the Kanab amber snail, and the fairy shrimp. Thanks to the Endangered Species Act, human beings are too often being forcibly sacrificed to any plant, animal, or bug that catches a bureaucrat's fancy.

* It requires almost no evidence for the U.S. Interior Department to proclaim a species endangered or threatened. And once government bureaucrats have unilaterally made that decision, they can restrict the use of property in any area in which the threatened species resides—or *might reside.* Over eight hundred species are now on the endangered list, and thousands more could be added in the next few years.

* In Austin, Texas, in 1994, three thousand farmers and other Texans marched to denounce the Fish and Wildlife Service for its proposal to quarantine eight hundred thousand acres of land across thirty-three Texas counties to protect the golden-cheeked warbler. Property values dived by over $300 million in Travis County alone after the Fish and Wildlife Service designated much of the county as "protected habitat" for endangered species.

* The Fish and Wildlife Service designated one-quarter million acres of land as protected habitat for the California gnatcatcher in 1991. The Building Industry Association of Southern California estimated that that designation could destroy as many as two hundred thousand jobs. The FWS's action was struck down in 1994 by a federal judge who ruled that the agency violated federal law by refusing to disclose publicly the information that it used to justify its seizure of control over the private land.

* On January 12, 1995, a federal judge halted all mining, ranching, and logging on fourteen million acres of Idaho land in national forests. The judge took the action in order to protect three salmon species. The judge's action brought thousands of angry Idaho citizens to the streets to protest his action; as one speaker told a rally, "Our lives are about to be destroyed and disappear."

* The Endangered Species Act has made self-defense a crime. John Shuler, a Montana rancher, was fined $4,000 by the Interior Department for shooting a grizzly bear that was heading to attack him. Grizzly bears had been mauling Shuler's sheep for months. When he heard a disturbance late one night, he grabbed his gun and went outside. He saw three grizzlies attacking his sheep—and a fourth one heading toward him. The man shot the bear that was charging him, then retreated to the safety of his home. The Interior Department sued Shuler and the case was heard before one of the agency's administrative law judges. The judge held that Shuler was at fault because "he purposefully placed himself in the zone of imminent danger."

* On October 26, 1993, dozens of homes and tens of thousands of acres in Riverside County were burned as a direct result of policies imposed by the Fish and Wildlife Service. The FWS designated seventy-seven thousand acres in Riverside County, California, as a "rat preserve" for the kangaroo rat. Homeowners in that area knew that the buildup of brush posed a grave fire damage, and sought to plow their land lightly in order to create firebreaks. But the Fish and Wildlife Service repeatedly threatened prison sentences and fines of up to $100,000 against homeowners who sought to protect their homes against fire hazards in the area of "protected" rat habitat. The Competitive Enterprise Institute's Ike Sugg wrote shortly after the fire, "The designation of brush as protected habitat—and restrictions on controlled burns and other methods to keep brush down—fueled the destructiveness of the fires . . . To protect the kangaroo rat from people, the Fish and Wildlife Service prevented people from protecting themselves and their property from fire." After the fire, rancher Yshmael Garcia complained: "My home was destroyed by a bunch of bureaucrats in suits and so-called environmentalists who say animals are more important than people." One homeowner saved his home by disobeying the FWS threats and using a tractor to create firebreaks on his land shortly after the fire broke out.

★ Federal agents can seize the assets of landowners, farmers, and others based on a mere suspicion of a violation of the Endangered Species Act. On February 20, 1994, dozens of federal and state agents descended on the California farm of Taung Lin, an immigrant from Taiwan. The government suspected that Lin's farming operation had disrupted the habitat of Tipton kangaroo rats. The raiders found what they were looking for: a few little rat bones. The Fish and Wildlife Service arrested Lin's tractor on the spot, hauled it off, and filed suit: *United States of America* v. *One Ford Tractor, Serial No. Md1VC715V.* The government also filed suit against Lin, seeking penalties of $300,000 and a prison sentence of up to one year. Eventually, the government dropped all charges against Lin after he agreed to some of its demands, including donating $5,000 for endangered species protection.

★ Fish and Wildlife officials show scant respect for private property owners or their rights. In 1992, the Fish and Wildlife Service put out a plan for saving the blunt-nosed leopard lizard in the San Joaquin Valley of California that called for effectively freezing thirty thousand acres of land in the valley for lizard habitat. The Fish and Wildlife Service's master plan declared that "conflicting

land users will be reduced or eliminated in an effort to restore
habit to optimal conditions."

* The most disruptive endangered species case is that of the northern spotted owl. Beginning in the early 1990s, the Interior Department shut down much of the states of Oregon and Washington, and northern California—throwing up to one hundred
thousand people out of work—in order to coddle this owl. The
federal government prohibited timber harvesting on private land
within a ten-thousand-acre radius around each owl. A total of
over ten million acres was economically iced. A report prepared
for the governor of Oregon concluded that the designation may
cause a long-term loss of $10 billion to the nation. The ban on
timber harvesting helped double lumber prices, thereby adding
roughly $5,000 to the cost of building a new home.

* The FWS's listing process for endangered species makes a mock-
ery of any concept of due process. Early in 1995, the FWS proposed to add seven mussels found in Alabama to the list of
ESA–protected species. Senator Richard Shelby of Alabama protested: "Scientific deception on the part of the FWS has gone on
long enough. Under current law, the FWS is the investigator, author, decision-maker, enforcer, and appeals court for all endangered species. That is very similar to hiring one person to serve
your county as the police officer, prosecutor, defense lawyer,
judge, jury, and appeals court." Shelby complained: "I firmly believe that the FWS has little valid scientific information about
the location, history, population status, life cycle needs, and host
fish requirements of these mussels, as well as the activities which
adversely affect them."

THE CRA:

Federally Sponsored
Urban Terrorism

Federal agencies are forcing banks to make more bad loans to politically preferred clients. Politicians are acting as if they should have unlimited control over the operation of private banks and thrifts. The Community Reinvestment Act, enacted in 1977, was supposed to prevent banks from taking deposits in one neighborhood and making loans in other neighborhoods. But politicians and ambitious bureaucrats have continually expanded the reach of the law.

Since President Clinton took office, the federal government has practically ignored the law and resorted to sheer coercion and threats against banks to force them to loan more to favored groups. As former assistant treasury secretary Paul Craig Roberts observed, "The Justice Department is simply trying to establish by consent decree a system of racial quotas in lending regardless of credit risks."

Clinton administration officials claim that the CRA and other banking laws require that banks follow fair lending policies. "Fair lending" is a vague term, presumably referring to treating potential borrowers equally. But this is the last thing that politicians have in mind. To them, "fair lending" means losing sufficient money to satisfy politicians and political activists. The essence of fair lending has become a political shakedown in the name of social justice. Even though failures by federally insured banks and savings and loans have cost taxpayers more than $200 billion since 1980, the main problem that Washington now sees is that not enough risky loans are being made.

Federal banking agencies have been doing CRA oversight examinations of banks for almost twenty years. Federal examiners visit banks and examine their loan files and records of community outreach and support to determine whether they have satisfied their CRA requirements. In recent years, out of 12,000 banks examined, only 2 percent—or 240 banks—had CRA ratings of "needs to improve" or "substantial noncompliance." Thus, the vast majority of banks have satisfied the requirements of the law that Congress actually wrote.

But, even if a bank has a satisfactory CRA rating, community groups can use federal regulatory procedures to shake it down.

★ In order to get government approval to open a new branch—or sometimes even to open a new ATM machine—or to merge with some other bank, a bank must effectively get approval from community activist groups. Many of these groups are explicit about their goal; Bruce Marks, executive director of Union Neighborhood Assistance Corporation in New York City, describes himself as an "urban terrorist."

One of the most active organizations nationwide is the Association of Community Organizations for Reform Now—known by its acronym, ACORN. As Doug Bandow, a Cato Institute analyst and author of *The Politics of Envy*, notes, "ACORN and its allies usually demand money for the protesting organization, below-market interest rates on loans to businesses run by ACORN and its officers, low-interest loans, controlled by ACORN, in poor areas, minority hiring quotas, and cheap banking service for selected groups." ACORN agents were denounced in Washington, D.C., in 1992, for demanding cash contributions from shop owners and threatened them with picketing and boycotts unless they bankrolled an ACORN project.

★ Federal CRA regulations invite extortionate demands by community groups. Jonathan Macey, a professor at Cornell University

Law School, observed, "You see really weird things when you look at the Code of Federal Regulations . . . like federal regulators are encouraged to leave the room and allow community groups to negotiate ex parte with bankers in a community reinvestment context. . . . Giving jobs to the top five officials of these community or shakedown groups is generally high up on the list [of demands]. So, what we really have is a bit of old world Sicily brought into the U.S., but legitimized and given the patina of government support." Edward Crutchfield, chairman of the First Union Corporation, one of the nation's fastest-growing financial organizations, denounced the CRA process as "pure blackmail."

✳ If banks wish to avoid federal accusations that they have not loaned/given enough to blacks, there is an easy solution. The bank can simply hand over its assets to the federal government via purchases of Treasury bills and other government-issued debt. As Macey noted, "There is a direct correlation with severity of CRA enforcement and banks allocating their resources to government securities." A bank can satisfy CRA demands simply by taking "some of the money you were loaning to white, middle-class people and invest it in government securities."

✳ Politicians in recent years have repeatedly accused banks of being biased against minorities. But a Federal Reserve Board study released this past January (1995) examined over two hundred thousand mortgage loans made in the late 1980s and found that, as the *Wall Street Journal* reported, "blacks defaulted about twice as often as white borrowers. . . . Authors of the Fed study said the finding undercuts arguments that lenders often hold minority applicants to higher standards than white. If that were true, they said, their study should have found lower default rates—since minorities would presumably be exceptionally qualified given the alleged higher standards." The study noted that "black borrowers exhibit significantly higher default rates in both urban and suburban locations," and that "losses incurred in the event of default tend to be greater on loans extended to black borrowers."

While politicians lambast banks' higher rejection rate of black loan applicants as racism, minority-owned banks reject loan ap-

plications from blacks three times more often than they reject
loan applications from Asian borrowers, and more than 50 percent more often than they reject applications from white borrowers, according to the Federal Reserve.

★ The latest definition of "fair lending" came in the settlement that
the Justice Department coerced upon Chevy Chase Federal Savings Bank last year. Clinton administration officials saw a *Washington Post* series on alleged bias by Washington, D.C.–area banks
in 1993. They responded by launching an investigation. Federal
investigators went through thousands of loan files and did not
find a single case in which Chevy Chase had discriminated
against a black loan applicant. Instead of admitting that the bank
was innocent under established law, however, the U.S. Justice Department invented new rules and announced that the bank was
guilty for not complying with rules that had never even been promulgated by federal enforcers.

The Justice Department announced that the Montgomery
County, Maryland, savings and loan was guilty because it did not
pursue and bankroll potential black borrowers in neighboring
Washington, D.C., and Prince George's County, Maryland.

The Justice Department condemned Chevy Chase for not open-
ing any branches in census tracts with a majority of black residents. Ironically, federal agencies had repeatedly denied the Chevy
Chase permission to expand into black areas. Chevy Chase had requested federal government permission to open a branch in a
black area of neighboring Prince George's county, and twice permission had been denied. The federal oversight banking agency
had been concerned that Chevy Chase might have a higher loan
default rate in those black areas, and that the losses from loans to
minorities could undermine the bank's financial health.

★ The Justice Department's settlement required Chevy Chase to
"open four branches in black census tracts . . . and to make loans
to blacks with interest rates at 1 percent less than the prevailing
mortgage rate." The bank was also obliged to give black borrowers a cash handout to help them with their down payments.

The Justice Department announced that the Chevy Chase settlement should send a warning to banks and thrifts that ignore minorities "in or near their service area." Jonathan Macey noted in the *Wall Street Journal*, "According to both Mrs. Reno and Deval Patrick, any decision to locate a lending or deposit-taking office in a predominantly white area must be racist, because it necessarily involves 'shunning' predominantly black communities. Under this bizarre view, restaurants, convenience stores and all other businesses that locate outside of black communities also could be said to be racist." Macey later quipped that, according to the standards used in this case, "It would be as though you would say that a Kosher Deli is really racist because all they're selling is lox and bagels. If they had a different menu, they would attract a more diverse clientele."

DARE-ing to Destroy Families

Drug Abuse Resistance Education (DARE) is the most popular anti–drug use education in America. DARE, labeled by the *Chicago Tribune* as "a darling of America's drug war," is currently being taught by police officers to more than five million children in more than 250,000 classrooms each year. Unfortunately, DARE programs in some local schools have resulted in quasi-entrapment operations that have resulted in the destruction of families and the subversion of parental authority.

The DARE program is the brainchild of Los Angeles Police Chief Daryl Gates, who helped devise the program in 1983, after which it has been widely adapted throughout the nation. Gates made headlines in 1989 with his suggestion that drug users be taken out and shot, and his moderation permeates the DARE approach to drug abuse. Federal, state, and local governments and private donors are spending roughly $700 million a year on DARE.

DARE America Executive Director Glenn Levant (a former deputy police chief) observes: "Our detractors like to characterize DARE as an 'Orwellian reality' or 'Big Brother' at work. These bush-league tactics are transparent for what they are: attempts to support various individual personal agendas at the expense of our children." Unfortunately, the real results of DARE's heavy-handed tactics cannot be so easily brushed away.

DARE officers are first and foremost police officers, and thus are duty-bound to follow up leads that might come to their attention through inadvertent or indiscrete comments by young children. After police win the children's trust, children sometimes confide to them the names of people the children suspect are illegally using drugs.

* A couple in Preston, Maryland, were sentenced to thirty days in jail after their daughter told a DARE policeman in her school that her parents had forty marijuana plants in their home. The daughter was named a hero by the local district attorney: "The child set the example by standing up for her rights. This is the most extreme example of when parents fail their children and family."

* In Englewood, Colorado, a ten-year-old boy dialed 911 and told the woman who answered: "I'm a DARE kid!" He asked for the police to come to his house; after they arrived, he took them to a bookshelf, on which a small bag of marijuana was hidden. The boy sat in a police cruiser watching the police bust his parents.

* In Clyo, Georgia, eleven-year-old Tony Johnson met police Sergeant Sam O'Dwyer during Tony's DARE training. After completing his training, Tony met with O'Dwyer three times and eventually informed the cop of a few marijuana plants on a corner of his parents' land near their trailer home. O'Dwyer busted Tony's mother on April 9, 1992; Tony was arriving home on the school bus as the bust occurred, but O'Dwyer had coached him to pretend that he did not recognize the policeman. Katherine Johnson, Tony's mother, later observed, "I don't think it was a lesson well learned from the education system to teach our son to conspire in a bust against his family."

* In 1992, the eleven-year-old daughter of a twenty-eight-year-old registered nurse in Chickasha, Oklahoma, turned her mother in for possession of marijuana; the mother was arrested and jailed. An article in the *Chickasha Daily Express* noted: "The daughter, apparently having had D.A.R.E. instruction in school, knew what avenues to take when confronted with a situation like this." The

Chickasha police stated that other children also reported family members for drug use.

★ Nine-year-old Darrin Davis of Douglasville, Georgia, called 911 after he found a small amount of speed hidden in his parents' bedroom—because, as he told a reporter, "At school, they told us that if we ever see drugs, call 911 because people who use drugs need help. . . . I thought the police would come get the drugs and tell them that drugs are wrong. They never said they would arrest them. It didn't say that in the video. The police officer held me by the shoulder and made me watch them put handcuffs on my mom and dad and put them in the police car. I always thought police were honest and told the truth. But in court, I heard them tell the judge that I wanted my mom and dad arrested. That is a lie. I did not tell them that." The arrest wrecked his parents' lives; both parents lost their jobs, a bank threatened to foreclose on their homes, and his father was kept in jail for three months. Darrin became so agitated that he burnt down part of a neighbor's house because he said he wanted to be with his father in jail. Darrin's parents later filed for a divorce, alleging that the strain caused by the DARE bust played a major part in destroying their marriage, according to their lawyer, Jay Bouldin.

★ DARE spokeswoman Roberta Silverman claims that drug busts that occur after DARE training are often unfairly linked to the DARE training the child received. But the *Wall Street Journal* noted in 1992: "In two recent cases in Boston, children who had tipped police stepped out of their homes carrying DARE diplomas as police arrived to arrest their parents."

★ While DARE officials stress that the program does not encourage children to turn in their parents for drug use, the details of the DARE program reveal why busts can occur. One of the DARE lessons that police give students in kindergarten through fourth grade stresses DARE's "Three R's": "Recognize, Resist, and Report." The official DARE Officer's Guide for Grades K-4 contains a worksheet that instructs children to "Circle the names of the people you could tell if . . . a friend finds some pills"; the "Police" are listed along with "Mother or Father," "Teacher," or "Friend." The next exercise instructs children to check boxes for who they should inform if they "are asked to keep a secret"—"Police" are again listed as an option. Apparently, the idea that anyone should keep a secret from the proper authorities is inconceivable—as if people have a duty to report to the government everything they hear. The federal Bureau of Justice Assistance noted in a 1988 report that DARE "students have an opportunity to become acquainted with the [police] officer as a trusted friend who is interested in their happiness and welfare. Students occasionally tell the officer about problems such as abuse, neglect, alcoholic parents, or relatives who use drugs."

DARE officers work hard to get the children's trust. Policemen sit and talk with children during lunch hour and play games with them during recess. Arlington Heights, Illinois policeman and DARE instructor Tom Morris declared: "We really build up a close rapport. After awhile, the young children are giving you hugs." DARE spokeswoman Silverman observes, "Anytime a child makes a disclosure [of parental drug use] to an officer, the DARE officer would be required like any other teacher to report that to the proper authorities or agencies."

Not only has DARE resulted in the destruction of families; the program has also been a miserable failure at deterring children from using drugs.

* A 1987–1992 study of DARE participants in Kentucky, financed by the National Institute on Drug Abuse, reported "no statistically significant differences between experimental groups and control groups in the percentage of new users of . . . cigarettes, smokeless tobacco, alcohol, and marijuana."

* A 1993 study by the University of Wisconsin examining fifth- and sixth-graders in three Wisconsin counties found that DARE-trained students had lower self-esteem and were more poorly educated on drug issues compared to a non–DARE group. As an Associated Press summary of the report noted, "The DARE

group failed to show improved decision making skills, one of the major claims of the program."

The federal Bureau of Justice Assistance, the research branch of the U.S. Justice Department, paid $300,000 to Research Triangle Institute, a North Carolina research firm, to conduct an analysis of the effectiveness of DARE. The RTI study found that DARE has been far less effective than interactive teaching methods aimed at discouraging drug abuse. Overall, DARE was found to deter drug, alcohol, or tobacco use in *only 3 percent* of DARE trainees. The RTI researchers concluded that this was statistically insignificant. Most of the minimal deterrence that DARE apparently achieved was concentrated on tobacco and alcohol, not on drugs.

DEADHEADS:

The DEA's War
on Music Fans

What do you call a Deadhead in a three-piece suit? The defendant. The Drug Enforcement Agency and local police are targeting fans of the Grateful Dead, many of whom follow the band from concert to concert. Cynics often joke that Deadheads should "Get a Life!" Instead, the DEA seems to believe that Deadheads deserve prison sentences long enough to destroy their lives.

Use of LSD—a hallucinogen—is widespread among Deadheads. Since 1990, arrests for LSD have tripled nationwide, and the vast majority of those busted have been Deadheads. Roughly five hundred Grateful Dead fans are serving terms for LSD violations in federal prisons, and up to four thousand more are serving terms in state prisons.

Julie Stewart, director of Families Against Mandatory Minimums, an organization opposed to harsh penalties for drug violations, observed, "In the last round of Grateful Dead concerts on the East Coast, there was a trail of people left in jail afterward."

★ When the Dead played in Louisville, Kentucky, in 1993, local police arrested 272 fans within two days. Some of the arrests resulted from local police scouting at night among campsites used by Deadheads to discover thirteen people using marijuana.

* When the Grateful Dead played at the Blockbuster Desert Sky Pavilion near Phoenix in March 1994, police swooped down and arrested 173 people, mostly for possession of marijuana.

* The attitude of the DEA and local police toward Deadheads is difficult to comprehend. When the Dead played in Atlanta in 1994, Atlanta police sergeant Leroy Williams told a local paper, "For the most part, the crowd is peaceful . . . no violence, no fights." Yet, Williams also told the paper that the Atlanta police were "locking up [Deadheads] by the busload" on drug charges. At the same time, Atlanta had scores of murders on the books that local police had been unable to solve—but chasing hippies in tie-dyed shirts was apparently more important than finding real criminals.

* Logan Martin was arrested at a Grateful Dead concert in Columbus, Ohio, in 1992 and sentenced to four years in state prison after police searched him and found some LSD doses in his wallet. Ohio law mandates that convicted rapists are eligible for parole far earlier than people convicted of possession of even minimal amounts of LSD.

* A New Hampshire policeman publicly declared that he routinely stopped and searched any car with a Grateful Dead bumper sticker.

* Deadhead Christopher Sia got sentenced to twenty-four years in federal prison as a result of being set up by an undercover federal agent. The DEA agents first arranged for Sia to sell five times more LSD hits than he otherwise would have sold—and then insisted that half of the dosages be contained in water, instead of on blotter paper. When Sia's sentencing time came, because the water containing the LSD was far heavier than the blotter paper would have been, he received one of the heaviest sentences yet dealt out for dealing LSD. Yet, the only reason he was selling such a large amount, and selling it in water, was because of the conniving of the undercover drug agent. Sia observed, "It is scan-

dalous to think that the government would actually use the weight of the carrier medium to boost my sentence."

* Nicole Richardson, a twenty-year-old college student from Alabama, was sentenced to ten years in prison for "conspiracy to distribute LSD." What heinous crime deserved such a harsh punishment for a young woman with no criminal record? She merely answered a phone call and told an undercover drug agent where to find her boyfriend, who had sold the agent some LSD. (Her boyfriend, who cooperated with the prosecution and implicated Nicole, was only sentenced to five years.)

* The purge against the Deadheads is largely the result of a quirk in federal drug sentencing laws. These laws, known as mandatory minimums, dictate that a person's prison sentence is determined by the weight of drugs that they sell.

LSD is usually sold in sugar cubes or on blotter paper. Federal prosecutors count the weight of the sugar or paper as if it were pure LSD. (The LSD dose itself is usually smaller than a pinhead.) As a result, a person who sells a single cube of sugar containing only 50 cents worth of LSD faces a mandatory five years in federal prison if convicted.

DISABILITIES ACT:

Bureaucrats on the Rampage

The Americans with Disabilities Act of 1990 has brought out the worst in federal bureaucrats and conniving lawyers and encouraged far more people to claim to be disabled.

* According to the EEOC, the fatter a person gets, the more legal rights he acquires. The EEOC announced in August 1993 that obesity should be regarded as a "protected" disability under the Americans with Disabilities Act. The EEOC's zeal has added millions of people to the list of supposedly disabled Americans.

* A four-hundred-pound woman sued Southwest Airlines for discrimination after a ticket agent allegedly ordered her to buy a second ticket.

* The ADA deprived some residents of Los Angeles of one of their favorite forms of entertainment. The city's Disabled Access Appeals Commission invoked the ADA last year to force the Odd Ball Cabaret to close a shower stall on the stage of its nude strip joint. The commission ruled that since the shower stall would not be accessible to a stripper in a wheelchair, the business discriminated against handicapped women. No wheelchair-bound women had ever auditioned at the club.

* The Federal Highway Administration, to accommodate the disabled, proposed a special waiver program in 1994 so that truck drivers could be blind in one eye and have weak vision in the other eye. (A judge shot down the proposal.)

* The Justice Department ordered the Washington, D.C., subway system to put raised bumps on the edges of its subway platforms to alert blind people. (The changes would have cost an estimated $30 million.) But the National Federation of Blind People opposed the federal mandate because it believed that blind people would be likely to trip over the bumps and fall in front of trains.

* In January 1995, a federal court heard the case of two women suing the Caravan of Dreams nightclub in Dallas. The women, both of whom have respiratory ailments, claimed that the nightclub had violated their civil rights when it failed to prohibit every other person who wanted to go to two jazz concerts from smoking. (A federal judge rejected their charges.)

* On the flip side, Margi Chong sued her employer, Columbia Sportswear Company of Portland, Oregon, claiming that they discriminated against her by requiring that smokers pay a higher fee than non smokers for group health insurance. As *Business Journal Portland* noted, "The suit asserts that Chong's addiction to tobacco gives her protection from employment discrimination under the ADA."

One unintended consequence of the Disabilities Act has been its effect on violence in the workplace. In a June 1994 speech, EEOC lawyer David Fram implied that companies should be cautious how they discipline employees who physically attack their supervisors, because the employee may have a mental disability which the company would be obliged to "reasonably accommodate."

The EEOC rules have created a dangerous Catch-22 for employers. A spring 1995 article in the *Employee Relations Law Journal* noted, "Many individuals who become violent toward customers or coworkers suffer from some form of mental disorder. Yet for an employer to be too careful in screening potentially dangerous persons out of the work force is to invite liability for discrimination under the ADA, while to be not careful enough is to invite tragedy and horrendous liability for negligent hire or negligent retention."

* In Maine, a Postal Service employee was fired after his supervisors became convinced that the man's erratic and threatening behavior indicated he could become unhinged, bring a gun to work, and shoot a few ambulance loads of co-workers and bosses. The man suffered from "post-traumatic stress disorder" and was perceived to have a "volatile personality." A federal judge ruled in 1994 that the firing violated the law because the supervisor's decision was based solely on fear that the worker could become violent.

* In Orlando, Florida, elementary school custodian Leroy McMillon attacked the school principal during a job evaluation. When the school system fired McMillon, he sued, claiming that he suffered from a disability. (McMillon swore that he had forgotten to take his thyroid medicine that day.)

* In Tampa, Florida, an employee brought a loaded gun to work and made threatening statements to co-workers and bosses, acting as if he were about to go on a homicidal rampage. Not surprisingly, his company fired him. A federal judge in Florida ruled that the company may have violated the man's civil rights. Federal judge Elizabeth Kovachevich said that the company should have tried to find some "reasonable accommodation" to allow him to continue working at the company despite his mental problems.

Almost any condition can be the grounds for a lawsuit under the Disabilities Act:

* In Petaluma, California, an ex-rock musician and ex-drug user sued the local government for refusing to hire him as a policeman. The rocker claimed it was a violation of the Americans with Disabilities Act for the police to refuse to hire an ex-addict.

* In Georgia, a woman was fired from her job as a police clerk after too many missed workdays. The woman sued, claiming that she was disabled because of a "stress disorder," agoraphobia; she argued that the police department was obliged to accommodate her fear of dealing with people.

* In Minneapolis, a policeman who suffered from diabetes collapsed into a coma while driving his police cruiser. The cruiser crashed, causing minor damage. The police department, concluding that the risks of further comas was too high, discharged the officer. The policeman sued, claiming that the department should have accommodated him and kept him in his job.

* A school superintendent in Hamden, Connecticut, was arrested and pled guilty to drunk driving. The man vanished for ten days, during which time the school board changed the locks on his office. He filed a complaint with the EEOC, claiming that the school's action unfairly discriminated against him because he was an alcoholic. The *Mental Health Law Reporter* noted the superintendent "agreed to drop the charges after the school board indicated it would pay him a partial salary for three years plus lifetime medical and life insurance benefits if he would resign. An attorney for the board said the employer agreed to settle partly out of fear that it might lose under the ADA."

* Multiple chemical sensitivities is one of the most fashionable and fastest-growing disabilities. The School of Social Work at the University of Minnesota invoked the Americans with Disabilities Act late last year when it banned anyone who was wearing "scented products" (such as perfume or aftershave) from entering one of its classrooms. (Two female employees in the four-story building claimed that the scents were traumatizing them).

* Exxon had to pay $5 billion in punitive damages after a drunk skipper on an Exxon oil tanker wrecked the tanker and caused one of the worst oil spills in modern history. Exxon responded to the catastrophe with tough new drug and alcohol standards for employees in safety-sensitive jobs. As Daniel Seligman noted in

Fortune last November, the company is now facing 107 lawsuits by employees claiming discrimination against alcoholics or drug users.

★ Bill Bolte, a wheelchair-bound writer, noted in the *Los Angeles Times* in January 1995, "The very word disabled has been broadened to the point where a shockingly high percentage of the American public can claim inclusion and many of those who can't are trying to find a way to qualify. A recent workshop at Cal State Northridge had as its purpose the instruction of professionals on how to qualify physically or emotionally battered wives for inclusion under the ADA."

★ *Chicago Tribune* columnist Mike Royko recently reported a case in which the EEOC demanded information from a private company as to why it refused to hire a man who claimed he had a microchip in one of his teeth that allowed him to hear and talk to other people far away.

DRUNKEN CHECKPOINTS:
Every Driver Guilty ...

Tens of thousands of innocent Americans are stopped each month at police checkpoints that treat every driver like a criminal. These checkpoints, purportedly established to target drunk drivers, have expanded to give police more intrusive power over citizens in many areas.

Police checkpoints to stop and check all drivers for drunk-driving violations have become widespread in the last fifteen years. As law professor Nadine Strossen wrote, checkpoint "searches are intensely personal in nature, involving a police officer's close-range examination of the driver's face, breath, voice, clothing, hands, and movements."

The checkpoints have been extremely controversial. In 1984, the Oklahoma Supreme Court banned such checkpoints because they "draw dangerously close to what may be referred to as a police state."

But the U.S. Supreme Court sanctioned drunk-driving checkpoints in 1990, and police have since expanded their use. As long as the car is stopped and the policeman is there, why not check to see whether the driver is wearing a seatbelt—or has his registration with him—or has any open containers of alcohol in the car—or has any guns hidden under the seat or in the glove compartment? And why not take a drug-sniffing dog and walk it around the car to see if the animal wags his tail—thereby automatically nullifying the driver's and passengers' constitutional rights and entitling police to forcibly search the vehicle?

✴ A 1994 *New York Times* article on a checkpoint established at an exit off the Connecticut Turnpike noted that the checkpoint consisted of ten officers and six detectives—"including one with binoculars watching for furtive movements by drivers approaching the checkpoint." The police had a Labrador retriever that, a police chief claimed, could smell seven different kinds of drugs, even those in pill form.

✴ According to a North Carolina government press release, a statewide "Booze it and lose it" checkpoint crackdown resulted in not only the arrest of drunk drivers—but also the arrest of 137 drivers for firearm violations and 636 for drug violations. The press release noted, "In addition to targeting impaired drivers, law enforcement officers will be keeping watch for other violations of the law." This is essentially a declaration by the police of their intent to do visual searches—if not more—of all the cars they stop. The checkpoints did nab one drunk "big fish": state senator George Miller, Jr., who had championed strict drunk-driving laws.

✴ A drunk-driving checkpoint set up by Florida police near Orlando last December resulted in sixty-five drivers receiving fines for crimes such as not carrying proof of insurance, not wearing seat belts, nonfunctioning horns, loud mufflers, and failure to have the correct residential address on a driver's license. Of a thousand people checked, only seven were arrested for driving under the influence. Thus, almost ten times as many drivers were fined for violations with no relation to drunk driving as were fined for drunk driving.

ENTRAPMENT:

Destroying Lives
for Cash Bonuses

Thousands of elaborate sting operations have been set up in recent years designed to entice citizens to break the law—and to destroy their lives after they are caught.

It is a federal crime to be unable to resist repeated government temptation or deadly threats from undercover agents intent on ruining your life. A 1982 Senate report on undercover operations condemned government agents for "the use of threats by police to induce targets to commit criminal acts" and "the manipulation by police of a target's personal or vocational situation to increase the likelihood of the target's engaging in criminal conduct." Despite this warning, entrapment operations have proliferated, leaving a trail of ruined lives, and occasional dead bodies, in their path.

* The Postal Inspection Service specializes in stings seemingly designed to turn normal postal workers into mass murderers. In Minneapolis, one undercover inspector took advantage of a mail sorter's depression about his wife's recent death from brain cancer to ply him with marijuana—and then got him arrested and fired. A recovering alcoholic mail sorter had Darvon pressed into her palm by an undercover informant trying to get her to start using illicit drugs. In Cleveland, over twenty postal workers were fired

due to the false information provided by two informants who also ripped off over $200,000 from the Postal Service. A Cleveland judge denounced Postal Service inspectors for lying to prosecutors to cover up the abuses. A congressional investigation of the Cleveland busts concluded, "Some victims' children quit college [because they could no longer afford tuition]. Some lost their spouses and their houses. One victim attempted suicide only to be stopped by his daughter." Postal inspectors nationwide encouraged abusive entrapment schemes because the Postal Service gave them cash bonuses based on the numbers of busts of their employees—a "dollars for collars" program. Congressman Bill Clay, chairman of the House Post Office and Civil Service Committee, declared in May 1994: "These are the kind of activities—illegal as hell—that the Postal Inspection Service has been involved with for the last ten years."

* A Nassau County, New York, judge dismissed charges last year against a teacher who had fallen prey to an undercover cop who became her best friend, her confidant, and her business manager and eventually enticed her into making a few small cocaine buys and then threatened to ruin her life unless she became an informant against a motorcycle gang. Judge Raymond Harrington observed, "The police chose to try to terrorize her into agreeing to help them."

* Police infiltrate public schools, pose as students, and entice other students to sell them drugs. In 1993, New Jersey school systems were pressured by the state attorney general's office to accept police undercover operations (called "School Zone Narcotics Enforcement Working Groups") despite protests of some school officials.

On February 27, 1995, thirty local and state police raided Osbourn Park High School in Manassas, Virginia. Marcia Higgins, a twenty-four-year-old undercover cop, posed as a transfer student and persuaded three students to sell her LSD. Teachers lied to students during the raid, telling them they were being held in their classes for two hours while a "drill" was going on. In reality, police dogs were nosing past all the students' lockers and police were pulling people out of classes for questioning, as well as arresting and handcuffing three students in front of their classmates.

★ Federal drug officials have enticed individuals to accept government money and a government-supplied airplane to fly to Colombia to pick up cocaine; when the person returns, he is busted. Houston attorney Kent Schaffer complained, "The government has brought in more cocaine than the Medellín cartel." Customs Service "controlled deliveries" accounted for over half of all the cocaine seized by the Customs Service in south Florida in the late 1980s, according to the General Accounting Office. The Texas State Highway Patrol publicly complained a few years ago that most of the methamphetamine they were finding in the state was being supplied to people by the DEA.

★ In Osceola County, Florida, local police announced last August that they had made the biggest cocaine bust in county history—two kilograms. But police later admitted that the drugs that had been "seized" were already owned by the government and had simply been handed momentarily to a motel owner targeted for a sting. A police spokesman explained that the reseizure of the drugs was counted as if it were an original seizure because it would help the county police appear more productive in their applications for federal and state antidrug grants. Besides, the sting gave the county an excuse to confiscate the motel from its owner.

★ The passion to boost arrest statistics leads some police departments to go into manufacturing drugs themselves. The Orange County, California, police laboratory began producing $10 and $20 rocks of crack cocaine in 1993 and, in the subsequent eighteen months, over 350 people were busted for trying to buy the stuff from undercover cops. The Los Angeles Times explained the rationale behind the program on October 23, 1994: "In Santa Ana, authorities said their stings are intended to make small-time buyers eligible for harsher punishments. Deputy District

Attorney Carl Armbrust said Friday that the reverse stings help officers build felony rap sheets against users who will eventually be eligible for prison sentences if they are arrested a second time. . . . 'I'm happy with what we are doing,' " Armbrust said. The program still has had a few glitches, such as when suspects swallow the rock they bought from undercover cops before they can be arrested. One local defense attorney estimated that 42 percent of all the crack sold by the police actually has been consumed before the bad guys could be busted.

* In Los Angeles County, undercover police sell fake cocaine in stings. Los Angeles Sheriff's Department spokesman Dennis Dahlman bragged, "We've prosecuted a few people under the three-strikes law"—meaning that the people could face life in prison for being caught trying to buy a few dollars' worth of phony drugs from undercover cops, since they had two previous predicate convictions on their record.

In Florida, a police drug-selling program got shot down after a court ruled that such stings are illegal. The Florida Supreme Court ruled, "It is incredible that law enforcement's manufacture of an inherently dangerous controlled substance, like crack cocaine, can ever be for the public's safety." Hundreds of drug convictions were overturned by the court's ruling.

* In 1994, a joint federal-state sting operation in California against alleged big-time drug traffickers suffered a minor glitch. The bad guys absconded with two hundred pounds of cocaine that the feds had kindly provided. (The cocaine had a street value of over $4 million dollars.)

* The FBI is carrying out undercover operations to the tune of hundreds a year. With such mass production, little details sometimes get overlooked. The *Miami Herald* reported in December 1994 that an FBI sting against Medicare abuse turned into a fiasco after FBI agents sold thirty-five Medicare cards to a suspected fraud operation. The FBI used the Social Security numbers of legitimate Medicare recipients on the cards in order to add authentic-

ity to its scheme. Unfortunately, the agency lost control of the cards—and, as the *Miami Herald* noted, "now they have a monster on their hands." Medicare recipients have been shocked and horrified to receive massive bills for expensive operations that they never received, courtesy of the FBI sting operation. One of the victims of the FBI's botched Medicare sting observed, "How can they let this happen to people they are supposed to protect? I had to play cop with the clinics myself, making calls to them and complaining to Medicare."

★ Government agents often get promoted based on their statistical performance—how many busts, how many years the bustees were sentenced to, how much private property was confiscated as a result of an investigation. With entrapment schemes, the more private citizens' lives a government agent destroys, the higher up in the bureaucracy he rises. But the rubble of citizens' lives should not be the stepping stones to bureaucratic success.

FDA DRUG APPROVAL DELAYS:
Wait Until You Die

For almost twenty years, pharmaceutical manufacturers, consumer advocates, and congressmen have been complaining about the Food and Drug Administration's unconscionable delays in approving lifesaving new drugs. A study by Tufts University researchers found that the FDA's drug approval process is a tar pit of delays. The researchers found it took an average of almost nine years for drugs submitted to the FDA to be approved during the early 1990s. They also found that most of the new drugs that the FDA approved were available in foreign countries before they were available to Americans. In many cases, the FDA approval process delayed the appearance of the new drugs in the U.S. market by over half a decade.

FDA rules and red tape cause pharmaceutical companies to spend an average of over $230 million for each new drug approved. Stanford University professor Dale Geringer observed, "In terms of lives, it's quite possible that the FDA bureaucracy could be killing on the order of three to four times as many people as it saves."

★ Sam Kazman of the Competitive Enterprise Institute, a Washington, D.C., think tank, estimates that eight thousand to fifteen thousand people died during the FDA's review of misoprostol, a drug that reduces gastric ulcers among arthritis sufferers. People

with arthritis take large quantities of aspirin, which can cause ulcers resulting in silent bleeding that kills thousands of Americans
each year.

✶ Twenty-two thousand people may have died while the FDA dal-
lied before approving streptokinase (a drug that dissolves clots in
heart attack victims), according to Kazman.

✶ Thirty-five hundred kidney cancer patients died during the three
and a half years it took the FDA to approve the drug Inter-
leukin 2.

✶ One hundred fifty thousand heart attack victims may have lost
their lives as a result of the FDA's delays in approving the emergency blood-clotting drug TPA.

✶ The FDA has an extremely timid, risk-averse approach to approving new drugs; National Cancer Institute officials have accused
the FDA of being "mired in a 1960s philosophy of drug development, viewing all new agents as . . . poisons." George Rathmann,
the founder of the nation's leading biotechnology company, complained in January 1995, "American leadership cannot survive
the incredibly slow pace of government approvals." The number
of FDA–approved new biotechnology drugs decreased 75 percent
between 1993 and 1994.

Handgun Grabbing
for Fun and Profit

Politicians are banning handguns or proposing handgun bans left and right. These attacks on citizens' constitutional right to own guns are becoming more extreme year by year.

* Federal, state, and local gun laws are often administered with open contempt for the rights of the citizenry. Democratic Congressman John Dingell of Michigan denounced the federal Bureau of Alcohol, Tobacco and Firearms as "a jack-booted group of fascists who are perhaps as large a danger to American society as I could pick today." The Senate Subcommittee on the Constitution investigated the BATF and concluded, "Enforcement tactics made possible by current firearms laws are constitutionally, legally, and practically reprehensible. . . . Approximately 75% of BATF gun prosecutions were aimed at ordinary citizens who had neither criminal intent nor knowledge, but were enticed by agents into unknowing technical violations." Democratic Senator Dennis DeConcini of Arizona observed that BATF agents "move against honest citizens and criminals with equal vigor simply because they have taken the view that individuals who are interested in firearms are either criminals or close to it."

✴ On May 15, 1994, six carloads of BATF and IRS agents swarmed into the Pennsylvania home of Harry and Theresa Lamplugh. Within seconds of coming to the door, Harry Lamplugh had a submachine gun poking in his face as federal agents demanded that he unlock his safes and gun cabinets. During the next six hours, the federal agents trashed the Lamplughs' home—smashing furniture, scattering papers, even dumping twenty bottles of Harry Lamplugh's cancer medicine onto the floor. Lamplugh is the owner of the Borderline Gun Collectors Association, one of the nation's largest sponsors of gun shows—an activity that the BATF frowns upon. Mr. Lamplugh later testified, "When I asked if they had a search warrant, their first reply was, 'shut the f____ up motherf____er; do you want more trouble than you already have?' with the machine gun stuck in my face. They then proceeded to tear my house apart." The agents refused to show Mr. Lamplugh the search warrant or tell him what he was suspected of. The agents confiscated all of the Lamplughs' business records, as well as their marriage and birth certificates, school records, insurance information, and vehicle registrations and titles. As *The Gun Owner* newsletter reported, the BATF had the affidavit that led to the search warrant sealed by court order, thus preventing the couple from gaining any insight into why their home was ransacked. A year later, the BATF had neither filed charges against the couple, nor returned any of their business records or the $15,000 worth of ammunition and guns they seized.

✴ On May 8, 1992, BATF agents raided the home of Louis Katona in Bucyrus, Ohio. Louis was a real estate salesman and a part-time police officer and gun collector. His father had given him an antique police badge; when the local police chief saw the gift, he demanded that the police badge be given to him. When Katona refused, the police chief made false allegations against Katona to the BATF. The false charges led to the BATF raid. A BATF agent roughly shoved Katona's pregnant wife up against a wall (even though she was posing no threat); the shock and rough treatment caused her to suffer a miscarriage. Shortly thereafter federal agents confiscated $100,000 worth of Katona's guns. A federal judge threw out of court all of the BATF's charges against Katona, and he is countersuing the agency.

* On February 5, 1993, BATF and local officials stormed into the home of Janice Hart of Portland, Oregon. An informant had told them that an escaped convict by the name of Janice Harrell was living there and possessed guns. When Hart arrived home from shopping, she saw her doors smashed in and agents ransacking her house, searching for weapons. Agents yanked her around and kept snarling, "You're going to prison, Janice!" She asked to call an attorney but the agents refused to let her; instead, they took her to the basement and browbeat her for an hour. She finally asked the agents if they had a picture of the person they were tracking; they did, and the person in the picture bore little resemblance to Janice Hart. They arrested Hart anyhow, but she was released after her fingerprints proved that she was not the felon they were tracking.

* On April Fool's Day 1992, thirty BATF agents came racing into the front yard of the Colville, Washington, home of Del and Malisa Knudson. Del Knudson was away at work, and his wife was busy bathing her baby. BATF agents handcuffed the mother and left the baby alone in the bath. They ransacked the house for three hours, demanding that the mother tell them where the machine guns were hidden or buried. As columnist-editor William Chesire noted earlier this year in the *Arizona Republic*, "There were no machine guns, buried or otherwise. A Spokane judge had granted the government a search warrant solely on the strength of a tip from an unreliable informant with a known history of mental disability."

* On December 16, 1991, BATF agents, local police, and a TV crew that had been invited along went smashing into the house of John Lawmaster of Tulsa, Oklahoma. Dozens of agents ransacked the house, destroying Lawmaster's gun safe, tossing his personal papers on the floor, breaking furniture, and throwing Christmas presents around for sport. Lawmaster was not at home

at the time of the raid. As *American Firearms Industry* magazine reported, "By the time he arrived home, the agents were gone but the gas, electric and water companies showed up claiming they were told to shut everything off. The only clue Lawmaster had to what happened was a note from BATF that read: 'Nothing found.' When Lawmaster called his local BATF office to find out what had happened and to inquire who was going to pay for the damage, the belligerent local agent told him that it was his tough luck. When told to come down to the BATF office, Lawmaster responded, 'Oh, I will come down alright. I'll come down and bring my attorney.' The agent replied, 'Well, you bring your attorney, and we won't talk to you.' "

* Disarming citizens can be fatal. The issue of gun control often comes down to a question of how much faith people should have in dialing 911. A 1984 national survey found that 94 percent of respondents believed that police did not respond quickly enough to their phone calls for help; 100 percent of blacks and Hispanic respondents stated that police should have responded faster.

* Polly Przbyl, a Cheektowaga, New York, woman, was murdered by her husband in August 1994 after police took away her gun. A few days earlier, she had separated from her husband and taken her children with her to her mother's house. Her husband came to her mother's house and threatened her; she brandished a pistol to force her husband to back off. Police arrived and seized her gun. A week later, she and her mother went to her husband's house to pick up clothing for the children; her husband stepped out of the house and gunned them both down. Tanya Metaksa of the National Rifle Association declared, "I'm concerned about the police predilection to impose gun control on victims. Mrs. Przbyl wasn't threatening anybody. She was reacting in self-defense to her husband's threats."

* Many local governments have sought to fuel a general antigun hysteria with highly publicized campaigns to give any person who turns in any gun $50, or a toy certificate or basketball game

tickets. Such programs presume that any reduction in the number of guns—regardless of who disarms themselves—makes society safer. New York gun advocate Gerald Preiser responded with a proposal that he claimed would do more to fight the real crime problem. Preiser offered to give two hundred rounds of ammunition to any convicted felon in exchange for their old pairs of sneakers. Preiser declared, "The chosen footwear of our criminal subculture are sneakers, which facilitate quick getaways after predatory acts."

HISTORIC PRESERVATION:
Dictatorship of Gadflies

Even if a person does not consent to having historic controls imposed on his house, he must bow to the preservation police. There are over two thousand state and local historic preservation ordinances—and they are increasingly imposing bizarre restrictions on property owners. Hundreds of thousands of Americans have already lost partial control over their homes as a result of compulsory preservation policies.

* The New York Landmarks Commission imposed preservation controls over the 1958 *interior* of the Four Seasons restaurant. Preservation bureaucrats prohibited the owner from removing two hanging sculptures, changing the long draperies, or modifying the restaurant's bar.

* The New York Landmarks Commission also banned residents of SoHo in Manhattan from planting any trees in their neighborhood. Why? Because the commission wanted to preserve the grimy industrial feel of the neighborhood that existed in the late 1800s.

* The same commission prohibits residents in many New York apartment buildings from replacing their old windows (even

when they are broken) with newer, better-insulating windows. Instead, the residents must spend three or four times more to install old-fashioned windows that satisfy the Landmarks Commission staff. In one case, even though the owner of a condo explained that the two offending windows were facing inside the building toward another building's wall, and even though there were dozens of other offending windows in his neighborhood, the commission made mincemeat of him. As the *New York Times* noted, the condo owner "felt that he was being talked to like a culprit, someone criminally maintaining unsanctioned windows."

* The King County, Washington, Landmarks and Heritage Commission slapped controls on the land of several people living on the outskirts of Seattle, and prohibited them from modifying any buildings on their property—including even rickety old outhouses.

* Historic preservation controls sometimes financially destroy their victims. In January 1991, the Washington, D.C., Historic Preservation Review Board imposed historic landmark status on the former President Monroe, a four-story ex-apartment building in a borderline neighborhood. The board hailed the apartment building as an "important" representation of an early "multiple dwelling" and affordable housing from the turn-of-the-century period. But nowadays, the President Monroe is simply a crumbling flophouse: the outer walls have collapsed after repeated fires. The building's owner had intended to tear it down and replace it with commercial office space, but is tied up in court battles stemming from the building's historic status. The continuing court battle bankrupted him in early 1994—but the preservationists' court victory has done nothing to transform the crumbling building.

* Ellen Uguccioni, historic preservation administrator for Coral Gables, Florida, declared, "We address probably every possible condition a person living their life could encounter. Every single

item that could possibly cause a visual nuisance or any other nuisance we attempt to regulate through our zoning code."

* In Arlington County, Virginia, people living in the "historic" Maywood neighborhood have bitterly protested being required to file an application with the Historical Affairs and Landmark Review Board and to obtain a Certificate of Appropriateness before making any changes to the exterior of their houses. One irate homeowner blasted the review board for using "storm trooper" tactics to try to create a "rich man's housing project." Dennis Foley, a resident in that district, ignited a major fight in 1993 when he sought permission to install wood-grain vinyl shutters on his windows. The review board insisted that he use wood shutters instead—even though they cost twice as much and require much more maintenance. Though the difference between the wood-grain and real wood shutters would not be visible to people passing in the street near Foley's house, the review board refused to budge.

* Historic preservation designations are sometimes used as a means to drive up housing prices—and to drive out poor people and black people. A federal investigation concluded in 1988 that an Alexandria, Virginia, designation of a large black neighborhood as a historic district "was specifically intended to displace low-and-moderate-income blacks . . . in order to upgrade properties and . . . to promote the rise of property values and attraction of new residents." The racial discrimination involved in the historic preservation designation was especially unfortunate because the targeted area, the Parker-Gray neighborhood, had long been a symbol of pride for many blacks. Eugene Thompson, curator of the Alexandria Black History Resource Center, observed, "Parker-Gray is very special. It's an important part of African-American heritage. It's a place where black folks felt a sense of togetherness, a sense of belonging . . . a place they could call their own" in an era when repressive segregation laws prevented blacks from living elsewhere.

* The Houston, Texas, Public Housing Authority has sought for eight years to gain permission to demolish a decrepit, vandalized,

drug-ridden public housing project on the city's western side. But historic preservation activists have blocked the action in court because, at the time it was built in the 1940s, the project was a model for barebones housing projects nationwide. Because the Public Housing Authority cannot gain permission to demolish the often unsafe housing, it cannot gain financing to move the remaining residents of the project to newer, better-built housing.

* A fierce dispute raged in Washington, D.C., in 1994 over the city's imposition of historic landmark designations on seven hundred buildings in the Logan Circle area. This is one of the city's most mixed areas—with yuppies moving in and upgrading individual homes in an often dilapidated, high-crime area that has numerous soup kitchens and homeless shelters and several distinguished old churches. Thanks to the landmark designation, building owners must request permission from the D.C. Historic Preservation Review Board for any changes or expansion to their buildings. Many of the social service providers fiercely oppose the proposal, since it will make it more difficult for them to serve their clientele in the future. According to Reverend Beecher Hicks, pastor of Metropolitan Baptist Church: "Our opponents have filed this application [to impose historic designations] to prevent such unhistoric activity as feeding the hungry, clothing the naked, and caring for children from proliferating in our neighborhood." The *Washington Post* noted that "the debate over the historic designation has become a fight between a group of mostly white, affluent residents who own houses around Logan Circle and a disparate cast of social service providers and black parishioners."

* The First United Methodist Church in Seattle has been engaged in a running battle with the city's Landmarks Preservation Board. Even though the state supreme court ruled in 1992 that the city's attempt to impose landmark designation on another church in the city violated the First Amendment's guarantee of freedom of religion, the city is still pursuing designation of other churches.

The *Seattle Times* noted that "church members want a more welcoming worship space. Remodeling could range from moving the pulpit closer to worshipers and expanding the vestibule, to allow people to mingle before and after services, to replacing all or some of the building with a new, smaller sanctuary." The church's membership has fallen by almost 75 percent, and the current church members can no longer afford to preserve the church in a style satisfying to city officials.

HUD's War on Free Speech

The First Amendment guarantees Americans freedom of speech. However, if you choose to criticize drug addicts, alcoholics, or rampaging homeless, federal bureaucrats may swoop down, seize your diaries, try to grab your life savings, and threaten you with lengthy jail sentences. The Fair Housing Act Amendments of 1988 added drug addicts, alcoholics, and the mentally disabled to "protected groups" covered by the federal Fair Housing Act. As a result, the federal Department of Housing and Urban Development (HUD) now claims that criticizing homes for those groups can be a violation of federal law.

Unfortunately, people who enter programs for recovering drug addicts have an extremely strong relapse rate. Roughly half of recovering alcoholics and 70 percent of recovering drug addicts revert back to the bottle or needle. And homeless shelters can impact more than a neighborhood's ambience; the crime rate in Elmsford, New York, doubled after a shelter opened there. HUD has filed or threatened lawsuits against dozens of private groups that have protested the effects of HUD handouts.

* In Berkeley, California, HUD in late 1993 issued a subpoena to three residents who had complained about plans to convert a

ratty-looking motel next to a liquor store into a home for alcoholics and mentally disabled AIDS patients. (The neighborhood already had seven such homes for alcoholics and drug addicts, and
the crime rate had soared in the past decade.) After a local zoning
board granted a variance and rubber-stamped the project, the
three had sued alleging a conflict of interest, since one of the
board members was also the president of the organization that
would receive funding for the alcoholics' shelter. A federally
funded fair housing activist organization complained to HUD
about the group's action, and HUD launched a full-scale investigation of the three. In November 1993, HUD demanded to see
any letters they had written to public officials or newspapers, any
petitions, and names, addresses, and phone numbers of anyone
who had indicated support for the group's efforts. John Deringer,
who lived next to the soon-to-be shelter complained, "We didn't
feel we had done anything wrong, but we were very, very intimidated. The threat was we could be fined $100,000 and jailed
if we didn't give them the information they wanted. It was
chilling." The three targeted individuals and their attorney
subsequently sent numerous letters and made many phone calls
to HUD, trying to get further information or explain their
case. HUD refused to make any response or to give any explanation of its threat, preferring instead to let the sword of Dam-
ocles hang over the heads of its targets, as Heather Mac Donald
reported.

LaVera Gillespie, HUD's regional director for fair housing and
equal opportunity, finally informed them in July 1994 that "evidence was produced during the [HUD] investigation that your
clients wrote news articles which referenced the mental disability
of the intended residents of the proposed project as a reason for
the denial of the project." A HUD investigator contacted the
three Berkeley residents, offering to drop discrimination charges
if they "agreed never to write or speak on housing issues again."

David Bryden, the attorney for the Berkeley Three, called a
press conference and denounced HUD. Newspapers raced to pick
up the story, and HUD was soon wishing the nation had a serious
newsprint shortage. The agency backed down.

* In New York City, HUD launched an investigation of the Irving Place Community Coalition, a group of citizens opposed to placing another home for the mentally ill in a neighborhood already saturated with such homes. HUD responded by demanding to see membership lists, memos, even the diaries of people involved in the opposition. Arlene Harrison, a member of the Coalition, said, "It was like Big Brother coming to your door with a hammer."

* In Seattle, a neighborhood group protested plans to use five buildings in one city block for housing for the mentally ill and drug addicts. HUD threatened to sue the neighborhood group and demanded that they sign a "conciliation agreement" that would oblige the protesters to contact fair-housing advocates before circulating any petitions or scheduling any meetings criticizing the subsidized housing, and to promise not to oppose plans for even more subsidized housing. The protesters saw this as a HUD demand for a complete surrender to the demands of fair-housing advocates.

   Seattle attorney Roger Lee, who represented the defendants against HUD fair housing accusations, observed, "HUD sends out investigators who are extremely heavy-handed. They knock on doors and flash badges, and the intimidation factor is very substantial. The thing is, HUD has no procedure for throwing out groundless cases. They proceed even if there are no facts to back up the complaint, or if even it's legally incorrect."

* HUD is also engaging in extensive vigilante action against newspapers. The Fair Housing Act Amendments of 1988 made it "unlawful to make, print, or publish, or cause to be made, printed, or published, any notice, statement, or advertisement, with respect to the sale or rental of a dwelling, that indicates any preference, limitation, or discrimination because of race, color, religion, sex, handicap, familial status, or national origin." HUD perceives many geographical references in home advertisements to be federal crimes: "References to a synagogue, congregation, or parish may . . . indicate a[n illegal] religious preference. Names of facilities which cater to a particular racial, national origin or religious

group such as country club or private school designations . . .
may indicate a[n illegal] preference."

* A fair housing organization in Pennsylvania sued a realty company for using the term "rare find" for a house it offered. The
house was in a black neighborhood, and the fair housing activists
claimed that "rare find" was a racially discriminatory phrase indi-
cating that it was rare to find nice homes in black areas.

* Long Island Housing Services, a fair housing group, sued a newspaper for permitting the use of the term *professional* in classified
ads. A spokesman for the group claimed that the word *professional*
was a racist code word.

* The *Chicago Tribune* noted in 1994, "Realty professionals in various
parts of the country say they have been told 'walk-in closet' is un-
acceptable because it discriminates against wheelchair-bound persons, and 'master bedroom' is verboten because it suggests
slavery."

* Fair housing regulations are severely muzzling real estate sales-
men. The *New York Times* noted in December 1993: "Anyone
shopping for a house these days is likely to find brokers reluctant
to answer the question of which community has the best schools,
particularly in metropolitan suburbs. While this is a major concern of a buyer, brokers know that an inappropriate answer could
be considered a violation of the Fair Housing Law." The Westchester County, New York, Board of Realtors discourages its
members from giving out average Scholastic Aptitude Test scores
of local schools even though the figures are published in the newspaper. Board attorney Edward Sumber observed, "There is some
feeling that high SAT levels imply a non–racially mixed area."

* The Iowa Civil Rights Commission announced that the state's
newspapers were violating the state Fair Housing Act when they
published classified rental ads that specified male or female pref-
erences for a roommate. The new policy sparked fierce protests

from females who were subsequently bombarded with unwanted calls from males seeking to move in. The commission backed away from the policy last year after widespread public protest and ridicule.

THE IRS:

Our Tax Lynch Laws

The IRS has the power to destroy your life—even if you have violated no tax law and paid all your taxes.

A Gallup Poll released in 1994 found that two-thirds of Americans believes that the IRS abuses its power. Yet few people realize exactly how much arbitrary power politicians and judges have granted IRS agents over other Americans.

The IRS has disrupted tens of thousands of people's lives in recent years by wrongfully seizing their paychecks and bank accounts. Since 1980, the number of IRS seizures of paychecks and accounts (levies) has more than doubled—exceeding two and a half million seizures per year. The IRS can seize your bank account or paycheck without a court order—often based only on a clerical error by an IRS bureaucrat, accounting to the General Accounting Office. This means that, regardless of how hard you try to comply with tax laws, the feds might still confiscate your savings. IRS employees too often abuse their power.

★ An IRS employee in Boston pleaded guilty to extortion in 1992 after he left threatening messages on a taxpayer's telephone answering machine telling her that he would earn a $1,000 bonus for targeting her for an audit. The employee was found guilty after he harassed an ex-roommate of his girlfriend who allegedly owed her $65 for a telephone bill.

★ The IRS imposes almost no controls to prevent its employees from spying on other citizens' personal financial information. A General Accounting Office official testified to Congress in July 1994, "IRS internal auditors found that there were virtually no controls programmed into the Integrated Data Retrieval Systems to limit what employees can do once they are authorized . . . access."

A GAO report last October noted that the IRS does not even know the meaning of the words "taxpayer abuse." After the GAO did a report for Congress on taxpayer abuse, IRS Deputy Commissioner Michael Dolan complained: "We believe that the use of the term 'taxpayer abuse' is misleading, inaccurate and inflammatory." The IRS fiercely opposed a proposed system to keep track of the number of cases of taxpayer abuse. The GAO noted that the IRS computer systems are not even designed to "identify cases of abuse or taxpayer mistreatment from the taxpayer's perspective." GAD reported:

★ "An IRS employee, after a personal dispute with a contractor, gained access to the contractor's account without authorization. The employee then allegedly used the information to threaten the contractor with enforcement action in any effort to favorably resolve the dispute. . . . It was only because the taxpayer complained that IRS management was made aware of this specific instance of taxpayer abuse."

★ "A revenue agent [targeted] the returns of two taxpayers for examination against whom the revenue agent had initiated legal action stemming from a personal business dispute."

★ "A taxpayer complained to IRS that her bank account was levied after she fully paid her tax liability with cash. Internal Security investigated her complaint and determined that the IRS collection employee who she paid had embezzled most of her cash payment by altering the amount on the cash receipt he submitted to the collection support staff. The employee also embezzled other taxpayers' cash payments for which he had not submitted any cash receipts. Unfortunately for the taxpayer in this example, the situation was not detected until the taxpayer complained about the erroneous bank account levy made by IRS."

* The IRS is not shy about asserting its right to any expected gain by taxpayers. Last November, the IRS mailed a breathtaking notice to the brother of Mark Zwynenburg, who had been killed in the terrorist explosion of Pan Am Flight 103 in 1988. The notice announced, "In accordance with the provisions of the existing Internal Revenue laws, notice is hereby given that the determination of the estate tax liability discloses a deficiency of $6,484,339.39." Zwynenburg and his parents (named beneficiaries in the son's will) were given ninety days to pay the entire amount or appeal the deficiency notice to the U.S. Tax Court.

Yet the Zwynenburg family had not received a single cent in payment for the death of Mark Zwynenburg. A group of relatives and survivors of victims of the explosion sued the now defunct Pan Am airline and its insurer, but no settlement had been reached. The IRS simply made a "guesstimate" that the final settlement for Zwynenburg's death would be $11,702,925—and then demanded that the family pay up even before they had received the money. The IRS refused to back down even after it had been publicly ridiculed. John Zwynenburg, the father, groused, "I have to go out and hire my lawyer and my accountant to fight something that has no merit."

* The IRS claims a right to slap $500 penalties on individuals if they write only two words of protest on their tax returns. Laurence McCormick, a Brooklyn retiree, squeezed in the words "under protest" under his signature on his tax return filed April 15, 1992. The IRS promptly slapped a $500 penalty on him for filing a "frivolous return," thereby implying that the two words invalidated all the other information on McCormick's return. (The IRS

did not allege any inaccuracies in the return.) McCormick sued the IRS, and in December 1993 federal judge Jack Weinstein issued a rare defeat for the IRS's expansionary view of its own power. Weinstein ruled that the agency had violated McCormick's constitutional rights, since the First Amendment "protects the right of protest to any branch of government. . . . A taxpayer need not suffer in silent acquiescence to a perceived injustice." The IRS, in an act of extreme bureaucratic hubris, announced that the judge's decision was wrong—and thus that the agency is effectively free to impose the same $500 fine on any other taxpayer who writes the words "under protest" on his tax return.

MEDICAL DEVICE MADNESS:

Suffering for
Bureaucrats' Convenience

You or one of your loved ones could die because FDA bureaucrats are stonewalling, strangling, and evicting one of America's most competitive industries: the medical device industry. The Food and Drug Administration was created by Congress in 1906 to safeguard Americans' health; but in recent years the FDA is effectively sentencing people to die for the convenience of the bureaucracy.

* On April 18, 1989, FDA agents and U.S. marshals raided the factory of Earl Wright, seizing $300,000 worth of his Sensor pads—lubricated pads that women used to check themselves for breast lumps. Using Wright's pad—basically two sheets of plastic with a silicone lubricant between them—women can often find lumps so small that they were missed during doctors' examinations or mammograms. Breast lumps are a warning sign of breast cancer, which kills forty-six thousand Americans a year. Wright's pads were extremely popular with doctors, hospitals, and patients, and were widely used not only in this country but in Europe and Japan. Wright had submitted a request for approval to the FDA; the FDA was obliged by law to respond within ninety days, but did not. The FDA continually demanded that Wright do further studies—and then stunned him by demanding that he

prove that the pads could actually diagnose breast cancer. Wright
never intended that his pad be used to diagnose breast cancer,
since a biopsy and extensive clinical analysis of breast tissue are
necessary for that finding. The FDA crackdown, which has cost
Wright's company $2.5 million and which Wright is still fight-
ing, destroyed his business and the jobs of thirty workers.

★ In 1990, researchers at the University of Minnesota invented a
simple pump to revive victims of heart attacks. According to a
1994 study published in the *Journal of the American Medical Association*, the pump was almost twice as likely as CPR to save the
life of a heart attack victim. The new device was snapped up by
emergency medical service operations around the country. It was
so successful that France and Austria made it mandatory equipment for their ambulance services. Yet the FDA refused to approve the new device. Why? Because the makers had not done
extensive controlled studies comparing the pump's success with
that of CPR and other methods of reviving heart attack victims.
The FDA specifically insisted that the pump makers get the "informed consent" of anyone on whom the pump was tested. But
since many heart attack victims are clinically dead (with a
stopped heart), it is impossible to get their informed consent. Despite the pump's worldwide success, the FDA has decreed that
Americans should be prohibited access to it. One study estimated
that fourteen thousand heart attack victims who could have been
saved by the cardiopump have died during the two years the FDA
has delayed approval.

★ Dr. Richard Cummins of The American Heart Association estimated that at least one thousand lives were lost during the time
an approved heart defibrillator was delayed. The FDA prohibited
shipments because of paperwork delays—delays that have no rel-
evance to the safety or effectiveness of the defibrillators.

★ A June 1993 report by the House Commerce Committee found
that almost fifty medical devices made in the United States and
entangled in FDA review had already been certified for sale in Ja-

pan, Europe, and numerous other countries. The report stated, "Many of the small companies that populate the industry may be driven out of business altogether by regulatory delays. The process also means that Americans are denied health-care options that could be safer, more effective or less costly than those on the market today. . . . Doctors and patients in the U.S. face the daunting prospect of either having to travel to a foreign land to have access to the latest medical technology or having to accept a less effective and/or a higher-risk treatment for their illness in the U.S."

* Starting in 1990, the FDA has brought the medical device industry to a halt with an incredible regulatory logjam—even for products the FDA admits pose no threat to the public! FDA review time for major new medical devices has increased from 337 days in 1988 to almost 800 days in 1994.

* Eleven thousand American companies manufacture roughly half the medical instruments produced in the world, but are being driven into exile by foolish government policies. An American Electronics Association survey found that "40 percent [of device companies] reduced the number of U.S. employees because of FDA delays, 29 percent increased their investment in foreign operations, and 22 percent moved U.S. jobs overseas." The survey also found that "57 percent of the firms said the FDA had applied guidance instructions *retroactively* to some of their submissions," as *Biomedical Market Newsletter* reported. House Speaker Newt Gingrich has denounced the FDA as the nation's "number-one job killer."

* The FDA has been supervigilant in cracking down on medical device manufacturers. However, the FDA's definition of "medical device" is far broader than that of most mere mortals. Among the products which have been forced to gain FDA approval before being sold are:

   * McDonald's sunglasses
   * a wheelchair cushion

* an Amish country spa
* New Freedom Ultra Thin pads
* a dental bib
* a baby highchair insert
* a low-pressure mattress
* spectacle frames
* mint-flavored dental floss
* Super Poli-Grip denture adhesive cream
* a foot comfort massager
* a dental tray

* In June 1994, FDA agents swooped down on the headquarters of Synetic Systems, a Seattle company, to seize a potentially deadly medical device that FDA officials claimed posed a serious threat to the American people. The medical device? The Sharper Image Relaxation System, an exercise machine with enough bells and whistles to satisfy any craving for overpriced knickknacks. FDA compliance officer Darryl Thompson claimed that the machines were intended to "affect the structure or function" of users' bodies. Therefore, the producer was obliged to have them scientifically tested to prove them safe and effective. The FDA insisted that the exercise machine was so dangerous (even though there have been no reported injuries from its use) that it put it in the same category of medical devices as heart pacemakers. Synetic Systems surrendered to the FDA demands because it could not afford the hundreds of thousands of dollars needed to fight the agency in court.

MEDICAL MARIJUANA:

The DEA's Worst Nightmare?

Are you suffering from cancer, AIDS, multiple sclerosis, or epilepsy? Uncle Sam has an important message for you: Suffer.

Across the country, thousands of patients with cancer, AIDS, glaucoma, epilepsy, or other ailments are covertly using marijuana to treat their medical problems. Many have been jailed for seeking to treat their own desperate medical problems with marijuana.

* In La Mesa, California, Samuel Skipper was sentenced to prison for sixteen months in 1993 for growing a small amount of marijuana to treat his AIDS symptoms.

* "Barbara and Kenneth Jenks, a young Florida couple, are now deceased. Mrs. Jenks suffered from nausea due to AIDS, which she acquired from her hemophiliac husband, who had been infected by AIDS via a transfusion of tainted blood. Following the advice of a member of an AIDS support group to smoke marijuana to improve her appetite, she regained forty pounds. She otherwise would have starved to death. However, anonymous informants tipped off the police. Vice squad cops broke down the door to the Jenkses' house trailer, held a gun to Barbara's head, and confis-

cated their two marijuana plants," as Steven Duke and Albert Gross related in their book *America's Longest War*.

* The persecution of sick marijuana users can have tragic results. The *Orlando Sentinel* reported in 1991,

> Vince Hathaway said he smoked marijuana to endure chemotherapy for the cancer killing him. By the time he committed suicide in December, his family had been branded as drug users, watched by police and taken to court. Betty Hathaway says her 26-year-old husband was tormented by the trouble he caused her and their two sons, Jeremy, 6, and Jed, 3. He shot himself on her 30th birthday. She believes he just wanted their troubles to end. "That is what he gave me for my birthday," the widow said. "I would not have to worry anymore." But Betty Hathaway still worries. Because of her husband's suicide and her marijuana conviction during his illness, the state Department of Health and Rehabilitative Services is threatening to take custody of Jeremy and Jed.

* Jimmie Montgomery, of Beckham County, Oklahoma, has been paralyzed for twenty years after a severe auto accident. Montgomery suffered from severe scoliosis (an improper alignment of the spine) and severe muscle spasms. He had over twenty-seven surgical operations in the last twenty years. Montgomery smoked marijuana to help control the spasms and the pain. The police raided his home in 1992. After they found two ounces of marijuana and two Colt revolvers under his pillow, he was sentenced to life in prison.

* Jerome Mensch, a forty-three-year-old HIV-positive farmer in Charles County, Maryland, was arrested in October 1994. Police had heard from an informant that he was using marijuana on a regular basis. Mensch, who was taking antiviral drugs with harsh side effects at the time, never denied the charge. He said, "I looked in the mirror . . . I looked like I was just slipping away." But by smoking a few marijuana cigarettes a week, he regained weight and perhaps postponed the onset of AIDS.

* In 2737 B.C., Chinese doctors wrote about the use of marijuana for medicinal purposes. Harvard professor of psychiatry Lester Grinspoon notes, "Between 1839 and 1900, more than a hundred articles on the therapeutic uses of marijuana appeared in scientific journals. As late as 1937 extract of cannabis was still a legitimate medicine marketed by drug companies." The American Medical Association testified at hearings that year urging that marijuana not be effectively banned. Unfortunately, Congress—bowing to the exhortations of the Federal Bureau of Narcotics—proclaimed in 1937 that marijuana had no medical value. But the simple fact that a majority of congressmen say something, doesn't make it true. In recent years, marijuana has helped hundreds of thousands of Americans in their darkest hours.

* CANCER Scientists and doctors have long recognized that marijuana has special benefits not provided by other drugs—especially for people suffering from the effects of chemotherapy. A 1991 survey by researchers at Harvard found that 44 percent of oncologists (cancer specialists) have recommended the use of marijuana to patients to alleviate nausea resulting from chemotherapy. The survey also found that almost half of 1,035 cancer specialists said they would prescribe marijuana for their patients if it were legal. Studies in both the *New England Journal of Medicine* and the *Annals of Internal Medicine* have documented the efficacy of marijuana in people undergoing chemotherapy.

* AIDS Marijuana has long been known for giving its users "the munchies"—an overwhelming craving to eat. Marijuana's appetite-stimulant effect has been a godsend for many AIDS patients who suffer from a so-called "wasting syndrome"—the loss of pound after pound until they simply die. Many AIDS sufferers have used marijuana to help them gain back thirty or forty pounds—and add years to their lives, and a great deal more quality to their last years.

* GLAUCOMA Over one million Americans suffer from a type of glaucoma that could be treated by cannabis. As Yale professor Steven Duke noted last year, glaucoma is "a disease in which the force

exerted by the fluid inside the eyes damages the optic nerve. . . .
The disease is progressive, and for approximately 7,000 Americans per year the outcome is blindness." A federal administrative
law judge noted in 1988, "Two highly qualified and experienced
physicians in the United States have accepted marijuana as having a medical use in treatment for glaucoma."

✦ Unfortunately, the federal government has steadfastly refused even
to consider allowing any doctor in the country to prescribe marijuana to treat any illness. In 1972, the National Organization for
the Reform of Marijuana Laws (NORML) petitioned the federal
Bureau of Narcotics and Dangerous Drugs to reclassify marijuana
and recognize its medical uses. The director of the agency refused
to consider the petition. NORML appealed to a federal appeals
court, and the court admonished the agency for rejecting the petition without "a reflective consideration and analysis."

✦ In 1975, NORML sued the Drug Enforcement Administration
(the successor agency to the Bureau of Narcotics) to force the
agency to evaluate the evidence on whether Americans should
have access to marijuana for medicinal purposes. DEA held a
hearing, and a DEA administrative law judge found some merit
in some of NORML's positions. The chief of the DEA overturned
those aspects of the judge's decision.

In 1977, a federal court of appeals criticized the DEA's final order and ordered the agency to reconsider the evidence for the
medical benefits of marijuana.

In 1982, NORML petitioned the federal appeals court to force
the DEA to follow the court's previous orders.

In 1986, a DEA administrative law judge launched an extensive evaluation of the evidence. DEA judge Francis Young spent
two years conducting hearings and listening to scores of expert
witnesses. Young ruled in 1988: "The marijuana plant is anything but a new drug. . . . Uncontroverted evidence in this record
indicates that marijuana was being used therapeutically by man-
kind 2,000 years before the birth of Christ. The evidence in this
record clearly shows that marijuana has been accepted as capable

of relieving the distress of great numbers of very ill people and doing so with safety under medical supervision. It would be unreasonable, arbitrary and capricious for the DEA to continue to stand between those sufferers and the benefits of this substance in the light of the evidence of this record."

DEA administrator John Lawn denounced the judge's finding as a "cruel and dangerous hoax" and refused to accept the ruling. Lawn announced that the agency would only allow a given medical use of marijuana if it was an already "currently accepted medical use." And since DEA forbade any doctors from prescribing marijuana for medical use, that somehow meant that the agency must continue to ban its use in the future.

NORML sued again, appealing to a federal court to force the DEA to accept the recommendations of its own administrative law judge, and the court again compelled the DEA to reexamine the issue.

In March 1992, the DEA "reconsidered" and announced that it had been right all along, and that it would continue to ban any medical use of marijuana. DEA chief Robert Bonner decreed: "Lay testimonials, impressions of physicians, isolated case studies, random clinical experience, reports so lacking in details they cannot be scientifically evaluated and all other forms of anecdotal proof are entirely irrelevant." Bonner got warmed up and showed some of the fervor that is the pride of DEA: "Beyond doubt, the claims that marijuana is medicine are false, dangerous and cruel. Sick men, women and children can be fooled by these claims and experiment with the drug. Instead of being helped, they risk serious side effects." Bonner acknowledged that he based his findings on the same testimony and documents that had led DEA administrative law judge Francis Young to an opposite conclusion four years earlier.

★ Public opinion polls have found that over 70 percent of Americans favor permitting the medical use of marijuana. Thirty-five state governments have enacted resolutions that support allowing doctors to prescribe marijuana, primarily in conjunction with chemotherapy, to relieve nausea, and for glaucoma.

However, the DEA has promised that it will effectively destroy any doctor who prescribes marijuana. The federal government has preemption over state law on controlled substances, and since the DEA claims that marijuana has no permitted medical use, any doctor who prescribes marijuana will lose his federal license to prescribe any other drug.

✱ The DEA has recognized that some chemicals contained in marijuana smoke do have medical benefits. The agency claims that people should be satisfied to buy pills containing the active ingredient in marijuana (THC). But a 1988 study found that when smoked, marijuana acts on the brain almost immediately, while the pills can take several hours to begin working. The study, published in the *New York State Journal of Medicine*, found that 29 percent of patients not helped by oral THC did benefit from smoking marijuana. The *New York Times* reported last year, "Patients say smoked marijuana works far better than the pill does. They can control the dose by inhaling only as often as they need relief, and the drug gets from their lungs into their blood and brain immediately." Dr. John Morgan of the City University of New York observed: "It is absurd that we only have an oral tablet to treat vomiting. It's like treating diarrhea with a suppository."

MONEY-LAUNDERING MADNESS:

Structure and Perish

If you routinely take your paycheck to your bank and cash it, you could be found guilty of money laundering offenses and face a lengthy prison sentence.

In 1986, Congress passed the Money Laundering Control Act. The law was purportedly aimed at drug cartels who were smuggling billions of dollars of illicit profits out of the country. But while the act has been a miserable failure at deep-sixing drug cartels, it has wreaked vengeance on private citizens who often had no idea they were violating this arcane law. Representative Henry Gonzalez, chairman of the House Banking Committee, observed in 1993: "Hundreds of millions of dollars have been seized, but there seems to be little overall impact. Hundreds of billions of dollars are still being laundered."

The federal government now requires a Currency Transaction Report be filed for any cash exchange involving over $10,000 or, in some cases, over $3,000. The government's definition of cash is very expansive, including certified checks used to settle home purchases.

While politicians and prosecutors speak of the money-laundering statutes as the silver bullet to destroy the drug cartels, the laws have actually produced a pathetic harvest. In 1991, over half of all money-laundering convictions involved proceeds of less than $150,000.

While some federal officials portray money launderers as conniving, highly sophisticated schemers, most money-laundering convictions stem from such activities as simpleminded drug dealers getting a money order for a large sum of cash. Other cases involved people simply depositing a check from illegal activity directly into their bank account. A state legislator who deposited a $3,000 bribe check from an undercover FBI agent was nailed for money laundering.

Sting operations have been the order of the day on money laundering prosecutions.

Since the federal government has done a miserable job of enforcing its money-laundering laws on big-time drug smuggling rings, it has tried to make up for it by ruining the lives of average citizens who sometimes inadvertently break the law.

✱ In October 1994, a Chicago jury rejected federal charges against a Chicago currency exchange owner. Jerry Tufano, thirty-eight, a father of five, was the victim of an undercover federal agent for whom he converted hundreds of thousands of dollars into money orders in 1988 and 1989. The undercover agent asked that the money orders be structured in such a way that no single order would exceed $10,000—and thus, no transaction report would have to be submitted to the IRS. Tufano obliged.

The government waited four years after the completion of the undercover operation before it busted Tufano one morning when he was out playing basketball with his children in the driveway of his home. Federal prosecutors demanded that Tufano be convicted of "structuring"—but the regulations defining structuring were not even issued until 1989, after the end of the sting operation against Tufano. The *Chicago Tribune* noted, "The agent was posing as someone laundering drug proceeds, but the defense maintained Tufano never knew that. The one time the agent used the word 'drug' in front of Tufano didn't occur until well into the investigation, and she admitted she dropped her voice. Tufano testified he never heard what she said."

✱ In 1993, a federal appeals court overturned the conviction of "Uncle Bobby" McDougald, a Vietnam veteran who had been sentenced to eight years in prison for buying an automobile for an acquaintance. McDougald received more years in prison for allegedly laundering a few thousand dollars to buy a car than he likely would have received in some states if he had been convicted of stealing a dozen cars. McDougald had been befriended by a businessman, Ron Watts, and had obliged him by purchasing a car for an acquaintance of Watts with the acquaintance's cash. The car was registered in McDougald's name. Watts was involved in both legitimate businesses and illicit drugs. The government could not prove that the money that McDougald used to buy the car had come from illicit drugs. At trial, the government could not show that McDougald knew that Watts was involved in the drug trade. Watts testified that McDougald was openly opposed to drugs, and that McDougald would not involve himself in any transaction involving drugs. The appeals court found that since McDougald had no intent or knowledge of violating the money laundering laws, he was not guilty—after he spent two years in prison.

* One of the most important cases regarding court decisions on money laundering came from the case of dentist William Pickard and farmer Johnnie Hollingsworth—both of Arkansas. Pickard had failed at several business ventures before he decided to plunge $400,000 into buying banking licenses from the Virgin Islands and form Compagnie d'Investment de les Antilles Limited. As a federal appeals court later noted, the profession of international financiers was one "for which neither [the dentist or farmer] had any contacts, attitude, or experience." The bank was an absolute failure, attracting not a single customer. Pickard did what any good Arkansas dentist would do: he put an ad in *USA Today* offering to sell the bank.

Customs Service agent Thomas Rothrock saw the ad and decided to try to entice Pickard into money laundering. He repeatedly called Pickard and pushed him to launder cash for him, claiming to be a Mr. Hinch. Pickard refused to carry out one transaction Rothrock requested because it would be illegal, and repeatedly asked for assurances that Rothrock was not involved with drugs or handling drug money. (Rothrock at one point did tell Pickard that he was involved smuggling guns to South Africa). At Rothrock's request, Pickard structured deposits and wire transfers from Rothrock in amounts under $10,000, thereby evading federal reporting requirements.

Pickard and Hollingsworth were charged with violating the money-laundering laws, convicted, and sentenced to twenty-four months and eighteen months, respectively, in prison. A federal appeals court found entrapment and overturned the decision. Judge Richard Posner ruled, "Pickard and Hollingsworth had no prayer of becoming money launderers without the government's aid." Posner said the government's action had turned two harmless, weak, foolish, and (in Pickard's case, at least) greedy men into felons." Posner observed of the Arkansas dentist: "By the time he turned with quixotic persistence to international banking, he had already lost almost $300,000 in his business ventures. . . . He was a threat to himself and his family. He was never a threat to society."

★ Money-laundering laws are also being used to punish and suppress lawyers who represent accused drug dealers and other bigtime criminals. The IRS now requires that lawyers file a Form 8300 listing the identity of and the amount paid by any client who pays them over $10,000 in cash. Ten state bar associations have advised lawyers against making such disclosures, stating that it would be a violation of the lawyers' confidential relationship to his client. Federal judge Patrick Kelly struck down the regulations, ruling, "The attorney-client relationship is a sacred trust and should not be intruded in. . . . If and when a client consults with an attorney, retaining him for whatever purpose, the canons mandate the client's very identify must be preserved." However, other federal judges have upheld the IRS demands for lawyers to identify cash-paying clients, and the IRS has officially announced that it will follow a policy of nonacquiescence regarding Kelly's ruling.

★ A 1992 U.S. Sentencing Commission report concluded that some penalties imposed on innocent or inadvertent violators of money-laundering laws were excessive. But the report noted, "When asked about the comparative seriousness of offenses that involve 'clean money'—i.e., not criminally derived—and offenses that involve 'dirty money,' Treasury department officials took the position that both are equally serious if they prevent the Treasury from having an accurate data base regarding the flow of large amounts of money."

★ The sheer bulk of reports coming in on money-laundering violations may partly explain why U.S. government officials inexcusably failed for years to catch one of the most vile traitors in recent years—Aldrich Ames, the CIA agent who became a Soviet spy. Ames received massive cash payments and cash wire transfers from the Soviets, and later the Russian government, from 1985 to 1993. Ames received so many massive cash transmissions that he bought a half-million-dollar home, cash on the barrelhead. In 1990, Ames received three separate payments of $50,000 each— large wire cash transmissions from Switzerland. Dominion Bank of Virginia filed a suspicious transaction report (sort of a currency transaction report with alarm bells) with the Treasury Department—but neither Treasury, nor the FBI, nor the CIA paid any attention. As *Money Laundering Alert* noted, "Prompt attention to the Suspicious Transaction Report could possibly have saved the lives of some U.S. double agents that Ames betrayed." Several CIA employees tried to warn their superiors that Ames's living standard was suspiciously skyrocketing. The CIA investigated Ames's finances—but apparently failed to check for the suspicious transaction reports or other reports that would indicate Ames was laundering money. While the FBI and other agencies were devoting massive resources to undercover money-laundering stings, they totally neglected the stark evidence of the guilt of one of the biggest spies in recent U.S. history.

NO-KNOCK RAIDS:

Tyranny American Style

No-knock police raids are on the rise, ravaging American homes and destroying your right to privacy and safety. Today, an unsubstantiated assertion by an anonymous government informant can result in police sending concussion grenades through your windows and battering down your front door.

Early American courts recognized that law officers were obliged to knock and announce their purpose before entering a private citizen's home. American law was built on the English common law. In a landmark 1603 case, an English court decreed: "In all cases where the King is party, the sheriff . . . ought first to signify the cause of his coming, and make request to open the doors." Unfortunately, contemporary law enforcement practices, driven by hysteria over crime, have turned back the constitutional clock hundreds of years.

★ At four a.m. on July 13, 1994, BATF agents smashed into the apartment of Monique Montgomery, aged twenty-one, in Saint Louis. The BATF later claimed it was searching for drugs and guns; no drugs were found. Montgomery was startled—as BATF agents intended she would be, raiding in the middle of the night. Two agents held high-intensity lights on her, effectively blinding the rudely awakened woman. National Rifle Association counsel

Joseph Phillips observed, "Hearing such a commotion and being startled as anyone would with such a bizarre scene at four in the morning, Miss Montgomery did what most reasonable Americans would do. She armed herself with a firearm she lawfully owned for personal protection." Agents later claimed that they ordered her to drop her gun, after which a BATF agent shot the woman six times in the chest and hip.

* On August 19, 1994, Riverside County, California, sheriff's deputies smashed into the mobile home of eighty-seven-year old Donald Harrison and his seventy-seven-year old wife, Elsie. The elderly couple were in bed at the time the gun-carrying, black-outfitted deputies forcibly entered their home. The couple never recovered from the shock; he died from a heart attack four days later, and she lapsed into a coma a few days after that. Donald Harrison's daughter, Nancy VanDam, stated: "They were both just totally thrown off by this thing. There is no doubt in my mind that the raid is responsible for my father's death." The police expected to find a drug lab in the Harrisons' home, and were going on the tip of a confidential informant. The police search warrant stated that the officers were looking for a mobile home surrounded by a four-foot ivy-covered fence; the Harrisons' home had no such fence. The house targeted in the search warrant was listed as being made of corrugated aluminum, but the Harrisons' home was made of fiberboard. And the Harrisons' trailer was painted a different color than the trailer targeted in the search warrant, according to the *San Diego Union Tribune*.

* On March 25, 1994, thirteen heavily armed Boston police wearing black fatigue outfits smashed into the apartment of seventy-five-year-old Accelynne Williams, a retired black preacher. "Instead of four heavily-armed Jamaican drug dealers police found Williams, who neighbors said was so frail that it took him 10 minutes to climb the stairs to his apartment," the *Boston Globe* noted. Williams ran into his bedroom when the raid began; police smashed down the bedroom door, shoved Williams to the floor, and handcuffed him. Williams may have had up to a dozen

police guns pointed at his head during the scuffle. Minutes later, Williams was dead of a heart attack. No drugs were found in Williams's apartment. Boston police carried out the raid based on a tip from an anonymous informant who did not even give a specific apartment number; a policewoman simply took the informant's word, did a quick drive-by of the building, got a search warrant, and then got the go-ahead for her and her fellow officers to smash in the door. (Officers from the same unit of the Boston police had previously been condemned by courts for falsely claiming to have tips from anonymous informants to justify smashing into private apartments without warning). A *Boston Globe* editorial later observed, "The Williams tragedy resulted, in part, from the 'big score' mentality of the centralized Boston Police Drug Control Unit. Officers were pumped up to seize machine guns in addition to large quantities of cocaine and a 'crazy amount of weed,' in the words of the informant."

A subsequent police investigation sanctioned three police officers, including Lieutenant Detective Stanley Philbin, the officer in charge of the raid, who conceded at a hearing that he had read only the first page of the three-page search warrant. (Philbin refused to testify at the police disciplinary hearing of another officer involved in the botched raid.) After Philbin was hit with a thirty-day suspension, his lawyer, Christopher Muse, wailed: "Stanley Philbin has a broken heart because he has been treated so badly by people who should know better. They took a hypertechnical violation and ran with it to say that he is in some way responsible for this tragedy."

★ Customs Service and DEA agents, as well as local police, launched an attack on the Poway, California (a San Diego suburb), home of computer executive Donald Carlson on August 25, 1992. The government agents began their visit to Carlson by setting off an explosion in his backyard, battering through his front door, and seeking to terrorize Carlson into submission. Carlson, awoken by the late-night commotion, demanded to know who was at his front door. Carlson later testified before Congress, "I called out in a loud voice several times asking who was there. I received no response to my inquiries. I believed that robbers or burglars were attempting to break into my home and I was extremely frightened, especially when I received no response." Carlson grabbed a handgun to defend himself. It is unclear who fired first. Carlson was shot once, and threw down his gun as a gesture of surrender. Carlson was shot again in the back after he was down on the floor. Carlson later observed, "No one offered me medical assistance while I lay on the floor of my bedroom. . . . Eventually, paramedics arrived, and took me to the hospital. I was kept in custody under armed guard and shackled for several days at the hospital. During that time, I was aware of hospital personnel referring to me as a criminal, of police officers and agents coming into my room, and the like." Customs Service officials later claimed that they expected to find several automatic weapons and a huge quantity of cocaine waiting for them in Carlson's home, but no drugs or illegal weapons were found. The raid originated in a tip from a government informant by the name of Ron. Representative John Conyers of Michigan later observed, "Carlson was shot in the middle of the night because law enforcement agents relied upon faulty information from an informant, who was paid a percentage of assets to be seized."

Customs officials had Carlson's home staked out long before they launched their assault. According to the official affidavit, Carlson's home was a vacant drug storehouse; though the agents realized that Carlson was living an outwardly normal life, they smashed into his home anyway. The informant had said the house was a two-story dwelling, but Carlson's house had only a single level. Carlson arrived home at ten P.M. that evening, and could easily have been questioned and arrested at that time; instead, agents let him settle in and go to sleep before they barged in at midnight. A confidential DEA report concluded that the raiders realized that the informant had lied to them even before they launched the attack on Carlson's house. The raiders were apparently transfixed by the informant's claim that there were twenty-five hundred pounds of cocaine in the house. Carlson's lawyer, R. J. Coughlan, commented in December 1994 that once the informant "held out the carrot of the largest cocaine haul in the history of San Diego, they [federal agents] were blinded."

* On November 12, 1993, 170 National Guardsmen, police officers, and sheriff's deputies, backed by twenty Humvee military vehicles, smashed into seven homes in East Eaton and Greeley, Colorado. The attack on one Greeley mobile home began when SWAT team members blew the door lock off with explosives and charged into the trailer at dawn. Juan Pablo Rocha-Gallegos, twenty-two, was asleep in a trailer at the time of the attack; a police officer shot him seven times. Gallegos told the *Denver Post* that he was not holding a gun at the time he was shot, as his .357 Magnum was on the dresser. But a police officer claimed that he had pointed the gun at him as he charged into the trailer. (The policeman also claimed that Gallegos fired a shot at him, but experts from the Colorado Bureau of Enforcement concluded the .357 had not been fired that day). Local district attorney Al Dominguez said the policeman "would have been derelict" in his duty had he not shot the man (seven times?), since Gallegos supposedly pointed a gun at the cop. Gallegos was not charged with any crime; district attorney Al Dominguez conceded that it would be difficult to prove to a jury that the man was not acting in self-defense. (The drug raid was a huge disappointment; the raiders had expected to find a major drug ring, but instead found only scant quantities of narcotics. The *Denver Post* noted last year, "Deputy District Attorney Brandon Marinoff, who has prosecuted the drug bust cases, said in a hearing earlier this year that the fact that police found relatively small amounts of drugs during the raid means little. He said that intelligent drug dealers never have large quantities in their possession at any given time.")

* In April 1992, police kicked down the back door of the home of Adolph Joe Archuleta, age fifty-four, of Grand Junction, Colorado. Archuleta, who had been burglarized four times by people breaking in that same back door, came running into the room with a gun in his hands—and police shot him four times, killing

him instantly. Pitkin County, Colorado, sheriff Robert Braudis commented this past January on no-knock raids: "Such raids are very dangerous. They are the closest thing I can think of to a military action in a democratic society. . . . The 'war on drugs' is an abysmal failure, and even the term creates a very dangerous war mentality."

★ Robin Pratt, an Everett, Washington, mother, was brutally killed by a police SWAT team on March 15, 1992. Police came smashing into her apartment, seeking to arrest her husband. (A warrant had been issued for her husband's arrest, but a judge later concluded that the charges against her husband were false.) The *Seattle Times* graphically summarized Mrs. Pratt's killling:

> Instead of using an apartment key given to them, SWAT members threw a 50-pound battering ram through a sliding-glass door that landed near the heads of Pratt's 6-year-old daughter and 5-year-old niece. As [policeman] Aston rounded the corner to the Pratts' bedroom, he encountered Robin Pratt. SWAT members were yelling, "Get down," and she started to crouch onto her knees. She looked up at Aston and said, "Please don't hurt my children." . . . Aston had his gun pointed at her and fired, shooting her in the neck. According to Muenster, she was alive another one to two minutes but could not speak because her throat had been destroyed by the bullet. She was handcuffed, lying face down.

The city of Seattle settled a lawsuit on the case in 1994 with a $3.4 million payment to Pratt's family.

★ This past January, a federal judge in Boston ruled that the Lynn, Massachusetts, police had acted illegally when they smashed into the home of sixty-four-year-old Rose Zinger and roughed her up, handcuffed her, and dragged her down the stairs. The police had no search warrant or arrest warrant. The police did have a routine form requiring temporary commitment of Zinger to a mental health clinic. Zinger as a teenager had survived the Nazi holocaust by hiding in various places in Russia and Poland. Several of her family members had been killed, and she suffered from paranoia the rest of her life. An Associated Press story noted, "Relatives said her mental illnesses made her fear of being dragged away by storm troopers almost overpowering." The woman died of a heart attack minutes after the police assault began; a jury ordered the police department to pay her children $1.35 million.

* On May 1, 1988, Seattle police kicked in the door of an apartment in South Seattle. Erdman Bascomb, forty-one, was lying on the couch holding a television remote control clicker. The first policeman through the door saw the remote control and shot Bascomb. As he lay dying, Bascomb asked the police: "What's going on? Why did you do it?" Police expected, based on a confidential informant's allegation, to find a small quantity of cocaine in the apartment, but found none. When a policeman called Erdman's father, the first statement to him was: "What funeral home you want to take him to?" The family sued the police, but the city of Seattle has used numerous delaying tactics and, six years later, the legal responsibility for the shooting has yet to be decided.

* Even liberal states are jumping on the no-knock raid bandwagon. The Wisconsin Supreme Court ruled in 1994 that police could forcibly enter a home without knocking in any case in which there was "evidence of drug dealing." Unfortunately, "evidence of drug dealing" can be the uncorroborated assertion of a single anonymous paid government informant. The Wisconsin court said that the "possibility for violence" can be minimized by allowing police to rely on "unannounced, dynamic entry."

One reason for the proliferation of no-knock raids on wrong addresses is that the police in many cases is fabricating informants for search warrants. The *National Law Journal* reported in February 1995:

* "From Atlanta to Boston, from Houston to Miami to Los Angeles, dozens of criminal cases have been dismissed after judges

determined that the informants cited in affidavits were fictional."

* Between 1980 and 1993, the number of federal search warrants relying exclusively on an unidentified source nearly tripled, from 24 percent to 71 percent.

* Interviews with more than fifty judges and magistrates in Alabama, Georgia, and Tennessee found that none ever had required a law enforcement officer to produce an informant.

OFF-LABEL:
The FDA's
Dead-on-Arrival Policy

Pharmaceutical companies must receive formal Food and Drug Administration approval for each *specific use* of their drugs. Gaining such approval routinely takes almost ten years and costs hundreds of millions of dollars. After a drug is approved for one use, researchers, hospitals, and doctors routinely discover that the drug can effectively treat other medical problems. Such uses are known as "off-label" uses—uses that differ from the specific illness that the FDA has approved using the drug for. Donald Bennett, director of the American Medical Association's Division of Drugs and Toxicology, estimated that "60 percent to 70 percent of drug regimes used in the treatment of cancer and 80 percent to 90 percent of pharmaceuticals used in pediatrics are for purposes not yet approved by the FDA." According to AMA vice president Roy Schwarz, "In some cases, if you didn't use the drugs in the off-label way you'd be guilty of malpractice."

✻ In 1991, FDA commissioner David Kessler banned drug companies from informing doctors of so-called off-label uses of their products. Kessler announced that the FDA would enforce the ban with seizures, injunctions, and prosecutions. The FDA issued proposed regulations; then, though the agency never officially adopted the regulations, it warned companies that they would face its wrath if they violated the draft proposals. Kessler, in a speech before the Drug Information Association, warned: "I would urge all members of the pharmaceutical industry to take a long and hard look at their promotional practices. I do *not* expect companies to wait until this guidance becomes final to put their advertising and promotional houses in order." The FDA claims that once a drug company does anything to distribute information on non–FDA-approved uses of a drug, the drug becomes "misbranded." As a result, the FDA claims the right to confiscate all available supplies of the drug in the nation.

* The FDA's suppression of free speech could be fatal to cancer sufferers. The FDA's restrictive policies almost certainly result in more Americans dying from cancer. Brookings Institution analyst John Calfee noted,

> Cancer newsletters have been shut down. Symposiums have nearly been brought to a halt. . . . A leading support group for cancer patients has strongly objected that the new policy will keep patients from receiving the best therapies. Oncologists have declared that patients will die because physicians will not learn of efficacious treatments.

* FDA's censorial policies are also boosting the number of Americans who suffer from heart attacks. A 1988 study showed that the risk of heart attacks for males over fifty was reduced by 50 percent in men who take an aspirin each day. According to an article in the *British Medical Journal*, wider publicity of the "aspirin-a-day" preventative-medicine practice could save ten thousand Americans' lives each year. Yet the FDA has prohibited such publicity.

* Among the dangerous contraband the FDA is suppressing to enforce its ban are medical textbooks. Textbooks often discuss the latest developments in pharmaceutical use, including uses not yet ordained or approved by the FDA. Pharmaceutical companies often distribute free copies of textbooks to physicians as a courtesy

and sales device. But in March 1992, the FDA cracked down on a company for distributing portions of the textbook *Cancer: Principles and Practice of Oncology*. Last year, the FDA intervened to prohibit a pharmaceutical company from distributing free copies of *The Chemotherapy Source Book*—even though the company had already received FDA approval to purchase and give away thousands of copies. (The Washington Legal Foundation is suing the FDA over this policy.) The FDA claims that when a drug company gives doctors free textbooks that mention an off-label use of that company's products, the drugs automatically become "misbranded"—and thus subject to seizure.

The FDA's heavy-handed tactics are intimidating textbook publishers, who fear that including the latest information on drug use may result in the FDA restricting sales of their books. According to Kim Pearson, a former colleague of Kessler's on the Senate Labor and Human Resources Committee in the early 1980s, and publisher of *Food and Drug Insider Report*, "Several companies have abandoned plans to include the most-up-to-date drug use information disclosed by medical journals for fear that the FDA will restrict distribution of their texts in retaliation."

★ The vast majority of doctors do not subscribe to the *Journal of the American Medical Association* or the *New England Journal of Medicine*. Those journals often have articles that report how previously approved drugs have been shown to be effective in treating diseases or problems different from those for which they were approved. Under the current FDA interpretation, it is a federal crime for a drug company salesman to give doctors reprints of medical journal articles that discuss an off-label use of one of the company's drugs. Even though the medical journal articles are published in independent, authoritative publications, the FDA still insists that the distribution of the articles must be treated as equivalent to the actions of an old-time snake oil salesman promoting his latest baldness cure.

★ The FDA dealt a death blow to Lifetime Cable Network's Medical Television programming (which ran programs each Sunday) in an attack known as the Saint Valentine's Day Massacre. On February 14, 1993, the FDA's Drug Marketing, Advertising and Communications Division monitored all the ads on that Sunday's programming—and then sent out letters to pharmaceutical advertisers, warning them that their ads illegally lacked fair balance. (Companies whose advertising lacks such balance face having their drugs confiscated and destroyed by the FDA.) Specifically, the FDA regulators demanded that the companies include almost all potential negative side effects of the drugs being advertised—an extremely difficult task for short television commercials. The FDA even criticized one company for failing to include the page number where its drug is discussed in the *Physician's Desk Reference*. Lifetime had been running medical programs for almost ten years, for a grateful audience of doctors and their patients. Yet, as Jon Kamp, vice president of the American Association of Advertising Agencies, told *Advertising Age*, "The FDA killed Lifetime with a series of enforcement letters" that so "chilled the use of these ads that people pulled off the air like crazy." The FDA's action destroyed scores of jobs.

PILLORIED PARENTS:
Bogus Child Abuse Allegations

If you spank your child—or even do something as benign as restrict how many hours of television he may watch—government social workers may investigate you and threaten to seize custody of your child.

Parents nowadays effectively have no due process rights in retaining custody of their own children. Anyone can make an accusation against a parent to the government—and be guaranteed absolute immunity, regardless of how unfounded or dishonest the complaint is. Any government social worker can coach or coerce a child to make baseless accusations against his parent—and be guaranteed absolute immunity. Congress has created a system in which no one has any responsibility except parents—and parents have practically no legal rights!

* In San Diego, a social worker threatened to remove a girl from her mother's home if the child was permitted to attend a birthday party at her father's house. As the *Los Angeles Times* reported, "The worker advised the mother, who was separated from the father, to move to another part of the county and to keep her location secret."

✴ Trevor Grant, former director of social services of the Child Welfare Agency in New York City, resigned in disgust in 1991 after six years, and observed: "For the most trivial reasons families are destroyed. If the furniture is broken down or the house is messy, Child Welfare Agency workers will remove the child. When in doubt, the safest practice for the workers is to remove the children and then to file neglect charges that never have to be proved in court."

✴ In May 1991, a Prince William County, Virginia, social service worker absconded with a ten-year-old boy and left a note on his parents' door: "Chris has been taken into foster care. Please be in Juvenile and Domestic Court on Monday a.m." The son was at home after school without a baby-sitter, which the local government considered to be child abuse. When the social worker approached him he ran and hid in some bushes. The parents later told the *Washington Post*, "When he was caught, he refused to answer questions." The social worker concluded that the boy's behavior was proof that he could not take care of himself and carted him off to a foster home for the weekend. The boy later observed of his first night in the foster home: "That night I was just in the bed crying, because I missed my parents." Social workers permitted the parents to reclaim their son after they produced written proof that they had hired a baby-sitter for him for the time between the end of school and when his parents returned from work. (The county government made no allegation that the boy had been abused in any other way except being left to his own devices).

✴ Lesley Wimberley, co-founder of a parent's organization called Victims of Child Abuse Laws, observed, "More than 1 million families a year in the United States suffer false accusations of child abuse. Such accusations emerge during divorce disputes, personal vendettas or through anonymous hot lines. Children and families are devastated, some permanently. By accusation alone, children are seized and parents are denied access to their children—and to the evidence against them—prior to any juvenile court hearing."

In the early 1970s, the nation became far more aware of the tragedy of child abuse. After Congress enacted the Child Abuse Act in 1974, complaints of child abuse tripled, reaching almost three million a year. As Dana Mack of Institute for American Values in New York noted in 1994:

> This law offered special grants to child protective agencies in states where mandatory reporting laws were enacted. In granting full legal immunity to parties who reported suspected child abuse, and in making educators and health professionals legally liable for failure to report, mandatory reporting was supposed to stamp out child abuse once and for all. Instead, it seems to have fostered casual accusations of abuse. . . . A Florida couple was convicted of abuse for restricting a foster child's television viewing.

* A San Diego grand jury recently found that the local child protection system had "isolated itself to a degree unprecedented in our system of jurisprudence and ordered liberties." The grand jury found that the system had developed a mindset that child abuse is rampant, and that its structure and operation were "biased toward proving allegations instead of finding the truth. . . . The burden of proof, contrary to every other area of our judicial system, is on the alleged perpetrator to prove his innocence." The grand jury found that "some social workers routinely lie even when under oath in court," and that ample evidence existed of the failure of the child protection system: "But our lawmakers have for the most part failed to respond to such warnings . . . they are unwilling to appear 'insensitive' to the sufferings of children."

* On January 12, 1991, Denise Perrigo called a local community volunteer center to ask a question about breast-feeding, checking to see if it was unusual for a mother to become aroused while breast-feeding her child. (Perrigo's daughter, Cherilyn, was three years old at the time). The local community volunteer service referred her to a rape crisis center, where the volunteer she talked

to assumed that Perrigo was sexually abusing her daughter. The center phoned the police, who raided Perrigo's house, arrested and jailed her, and gave her daughter to social workers from the Onondaga County Department of Social Services in Syracuse, N.Y.

Perrigo was interrogated for five hours by the police. She later said that one of the policeman accused her of "having my daughter perform oral sex on me." Perrigo was formally accused of sexual abuse, including "acts of sexual conduct including mouth-to-breast contact." The term breast-feeding was never used.

Perrigo's case went before a local judge the following Monday morning, and the judge threw all charges against her out of court.

But rather than give Cherilyn back to her mother, the Department of Social Services immediately filed another set of charges. The daughter was placed in a foster home. The social workers effectively claimed that Perrigo was a pervert because she was still breast-feeding her three-year-old daughter. Yet, as Dr. Ruth Lawrence, a University of Rochester pediatrician and one of the nation's foremost authorities on breast-feeding, notes, the international average length of nursing is 4.2 years. (One policeman reportedly lectured Perrigo on the night of her arrest that it was "physically impossible to nurse after eighteen months," so she must be nursing for her own gratification, as *Newsday* reported.)

The case against Perrigo was heard by a local family court judge three months later—and once again all the charges were thrown out of court.

Yet, Cherilyn was kept in foster care, and social workers permitted Perrigo to see her daughter only two hours once every two weeks.

In the following months, Cherilyn was interrogated by social workers and psychologists more than thirty times. Five months later, family court judge Edward McLaughlin again dismissed all charges.

POLICE BRUTALITY:

A License to Maul

Police in many cities across the country brutalize, tyrannize, and pillage innocent citizens. Too often, their fellow policemen and supervisors look the other way—and atrocities remain hidden behind a "Blue Wall of Silence."

Unfortunately, when it comes to police brutality, politicians, judges, and police bureaucrats have miserably failed to protect the American public. While many police are bravely and steadfastly serving and protecting their fellow citizens, too many others are acting like public enemies.

★ In 1991, four policemen from the Oakland, California, Housing Authority were convicted for assaulting, robbing, stealing from, and planting drugs on local residents; several others pleaded guilty. U.S. Attorney William McGivern described the cops' behavior toward public housing residents: "They stole from them, they beat them up, they threatened and intimidated them, and their supervisors in some cases stood by and allowed this to happen." One local attorney involved in cases against the housing authority characterized the police tactics as "a planned terror campaign" that had victimized residents. The police abuses skyrocketed after they received a special federal grant to crack down on drug trafficking at housing projects.

✴ In New Orleans last December, U.S. Attorney Eddie Jordan announced: "I would describe corruption in the New Orleans Police Department to be . . . rampant and systematic." In the past three years, more than thirty New Orleans policemen have been busted for crimes including bribery, theft—and even bank robbery. The *New York Times* noted in January 1995 that the new department chief sought to "discourage vigorously two time-honored department traditions: robbing drug peddlers, and tooling around town in recovered stolen cars that officers never bothered to report as found." One New Orleans policeman found a decisive way to respond to a police brutality complaint. On the day after Kim Groves watched policeman Lynn Davis and a colleague pistol-whip a seventeen-year-old boy, Groves filed a complaint alleging police brutality. Davis responded by phoning a drug dealer he knew and arranging to have Kim Groves murdered. After the thirty-two-year-old mother of three was shot within blocks of her front door, the killer called the cop to confirm the hit and share a laugh. The cop who arranged the murder had, as one fellow officer observed, "an internal affairs jacket as thick as a telephone book. But supervisors have swept his dirt under the rug for so long that it's coming back to haunt them." The policeman had been suspended four times since his hiring in 1987, and was known as a "terrorist" by residents of a public housing complex he patrolled.

✴ Montgomery County, Maryland, police were embarrassed in 1991 after one of their own killed a woman with his shotgun as she was standing next to her car eating corn chips. (A judge sentenced the cop, who claimed the gun fired accidentally, to one year in prison for manslaughter). The director of the county police academy later explained that the police department's program of target practice and firearms training had been halted the previous year because of budget cuts and concerns about lead contamination of the air in indoor practice ranges. The conviction was overturned on appeal—but reinstated by Maryland's highest court.

✴ In 1993, federal judge Joyce Green condemned the District of Columbia police department, declaring that "the District's sys-

tem for investigating complaints of excessive force by police officers has been so ineffective that it has helped cause the behavior
it was designed to punish and prevent." Green denounced the
city for "maintaining a [police] complaint and disciplinary process so ineffective as to virtually constitute a nullity." One former
police detective explained last year to the *Washington City Paper*
how difficult it was for a bad cop to get caught by the Internal
Affairs Department: "You damn near have to come in, knock on
the door, tell them you committed a crime, highlight it for them,
then call them every day and remind them to bust you."

* Last January, a black Philadelphia plainclothes policewoman was
dragged from the scene of a domestic disturbance and beaten
with fists and flashlights by other police after her partner radioed
in a call for backup. Officer Adrienne Cureton, a six-year veteran
of the police force, observed, "I personally believe they saw a
black, they grabbed me, and they did what they had the opportunity to do." The National Association of Black Police Officers
held a press conference shortly after the attack to complain about
a growing number of police attacks on black police officers across
the nation.

* In 1993, the New York Police Department was embarrassed by
the arrest of Michael Dowd, an NYPD officer who was busted for
drug dealing in nearby Suffolk County, Long Island. Though the
police internal affairs office had received a deluge of complaints
against Dowd, they had always concluded that accusations were
"unsubstantiated." Dowd's arrest sparked the appointment of a
special commission (chaired by former judge Milton Mollen) to
investigate police corruption and brutality in the city.

Commission hearings revealed that in one case, three police officers led by a lieutenant ransacked two apartments in East Harlem, throwing women against the wall, ripping up carpeting, and
punching a hole in the wall. The police had no warrant even to
enter the apartments. In another case, a policeman was seen
shooting a drug dealer in the stomach while robbing him. One
cop testified early on in the Mollen Commission hearings: "Police
officers view the community as a candy store."

The Mollen Commission concluded:

* "We find . . . shocking the incompetence and the inadequacies of the department to police itself. . . . From the top brass down to local precinct commanders and supervisors, there was a pervasive belief that uncovering serious corruption would harm careers and the reputation of the department. . . . No one seemed to care" about corruption.

* "One commanding officer encouraged illegal searches and arrest charges as a means of bolstering his unit's performance record."

Joseph Aramo and Leslie Cornfeld of the Mollen Commission, the chief counsel and deputy counsel, observed, "Today's corruption is not the corruption of Knapp Commission days [in the early 1970s]. . . . Corruption then was largely a corruption of accommodation, of criminals and police officers giving and taking bribes, buying and selling protection. Corruption was, in its essence, consensual. Today's corruption is characterized by brutality, theft, abuse of authority and active police criminality."

* Perjury is one of the most common police abuses—fabricating or distorting evidence to justify locking up private citizens. A private citizen who perjures himself in court is guilty of a felony, and faces jail or prison sentences of a year or more. In contrast, police and judicial tolerance for police dishonesty is so extreme in some areas that police are sometimes not even prosecuted when they are discovered planting drugs on a suspect.

* District of Columbia superior court judge Curtis von Kann complained in a 1992 letter to the Metropolitan Police Department that "as the pressure to get drug dealers off the street increases . . . there is considerable police perjury in this court."

* In New York, the Mollen Commission reported that police perjury is perhaps "the most widespread form of police wrongdoing facing today's criminal justice system." One former Manhattan

prosecutor told the *New York Times*: "No one looks down on it. . . . Perjury for the sake of an arrest is accepted. It's become more casual."

★ In January 1995, NYPD commissioner William Bratton fired the department's top corruption official, Walter Mack, and replaced him with a police department "insider," in Bratton's own words. Mack was fired largely because of his vigor in prosecuting police for perjury—which many department officials felt should not be treated as a crime.

RECYCLING:

Criminalizing Your Trash

Petty politicians and environmentalist visionaries have conscripted tens of millions of citizens as sanitation engineers—all for programs that, in most cases, waste far more resources than they save.

Many states and cities have passed mandatory recycling requirements, both for businesses and homeowners. Public schools have jumped on the bandwagon. Residential recycling has increased tenfold since 1987; over six thousand cities and towns now have curbside recycling programs. This environmental boom is creating a major budgetary strain on local governments. While many people have been led to believe that recycling is cost-effective and saves resources, it is actually more wasteful. But, as the *Wall Street Journal* reported in January 1995: "At least by any practical, short-term measure, curbside recycling doesn't pay. It costs residents and local governments hundreds of millions of dollars more than can be recouped by selling the sorted trash. It requires huge new fleets of collection trucks that add to traffic congestion and pollution. And it does so at a time when landfill space turns out to be both plentiful and extremely cheap."

★ Shortly after Cincinnati opened a leaf disposal program, the city collection sites were struck by a crime wave: people dropping off bags of leaves during hours when the sites were closed. (The sites were only open on government employee convenience time—three to six-thirty p.m. on weekdays and eleven a.m. to six-thirty p.m. weekends). A local environmental officer told the *Cincinnati Enquirer* that people who dumped their leaves in bags outside the site's gates when it was not open could face fines of up to $10,000 plus jail time.

* New York officials set up special bins to collect the newspapers of commuters coming through Penn Central train station. Police arrested a Lynbrook, Long Island, woman after she retrieved a newspaper out of a recycling bin for a quick look during rush hour.

* Chicago began a new program this year that forces apartment owners to arrange their own recycling haulers, carry out an education program for tenants, and keep on file a written review of their recycling operation. Violators face $100-a-day fines.

* Los Angeles imposed mandatory recycling on residents in 1992. One result of the program: scavengers going through neighborhoods plucking cans and bottles from recycling bins. Marilyn McGuire, the city's refuse collection manager, observed, "The majority of the residents seem to feel that the scavengers are coming into their neighborhood creating messes, making noise, that they're undesirable, that they may be casing their places to come back later and burglarize." McGuire announced plans to crack down on organized gangs of recycling scavengers, but insisted: "We're not going to chase the person pushing the pushcart down the street, throw them to the ground and take their materials away from them."

* New York City resident Robert Kanter was surprised when his apartment buzzer rang and a voice announced: "This is the sanitation police." Kanter came out and, according to the *New York Times*, the sanitation officer demanded to know: "Did you throw this envelope in the litter basket?" The officer declared that it was against the law to throw household garbage in a litter basket. The

sanitation cop had found two envelopes addressed to Kanter in a litter basket she had pawed through nearby. Kanter denied placing his household trash in the basket; he suggested that someone had taken the garbage bag from his apartment house and carried it off to look for soda cans. The officer sternly informed Kanter that he faced a $50 fine if he pled guilty, and a $100 fine if he contested the fine and was later found guilty.

* The high costs of recycling programs are due in part to the inflexibility and incompetence of local government labor contracts. The *New York Times* noted: "When the [New York City] program was established, labor contracts did not allow the city to shift workers from the collection of garbage to the collection of recyclables. As a result, the city had to hire hundreds of extra workers to pick up newspapers, glass and plastic. Workers who picked up garbage had less and less to collect and thus could finish a workday in four hours. Only with the latest labor negotiations has the city been able to cut the number of people picking up garbage."

* While some types of voluntary recycling—such as newspaper drop-off sites—can be cost-efficient, curbside pickups across a city are far more expensive than most people realize. Lawyer James DeLong noted in a study last year for the Competitive Enterprise Institute:

> Recycling is itself a manufacturing process. It uses resources of energy, capital and labor, and produces wastes. Recycling is not automatically superior, as a matter of either economics or morality, to the process of manufacturing a product from original raw material. Collecting, sorting and processing trash is expensive, and the costs far exceed the value of the materials recovered. The reality is that municipalities that expand recycling must cut other programs to subsidize the effort.

SECTION 8:

A Wrecking Ball
for Your Neighborhood

Regardless of how hard you work to buy and maintain your home, the federal government may give welfare recipients lavish payments to move in next to you—and ruin the block.

The federal government is involved in economic blockbusting in thousands of the nation's neighborhoods. The federal Housing and Urban Development Department is using government handouts to allow welfare recipients to move into middle-class and upper-middle-class neighborhoods.

HUD is using a program Congress created in 1974—the Section 8 program—to provide subsidies to low-income renters. Section 8 currently gives $7 billion a year in rental subsidies to two million families. HUD Secretary Henry Cisneros is pushing to expand the program rapidly to allow more welfare recipients to move to affluent neighborhoods. Cisneros calls Section 8 "a wonderful mechanism because it gives people tremendous choice and mobility."

HUD Assistant Secretary for Fair Housing Roberta Achtenberg declared last year on National Public Radio, "We are compelled by statutory prescription as well as constitutional mandate to see to it that every American has open and free housing choice." But the only people today who have "free housing choice" are those who have

HUD vouchers that force other taxpayers to cover all or most of their rent.

HUD requires Section 8 recipients to pay between 10 and 30 percent of their income for rent, and the government picks up the difference between the renters' share and the market rent. But, in contrast to the way the IRS treats taxpayers, HUD makes little or no effort to verify Section 8 recipients' income or to insure that they actually pay their small share of the rent. (The less the Section 8 recipient pays, the more the government must pay.)

Section 8 seeks to end the stigma of being on welfare by treating welfare recipients like a privileged class. Unfortunately, few Americans can afford the levels of rent that HUD shovels out.

* On the island of Nantucket, Massachusetts, a famous playground of the rich, HUD will pay up to $1,749 a month for an apartment for welfare recipients.

* In Stamford and Norwalk, Connecticut, HUD authorizes rental subsidies of more than $1,700 a month.

* In Westchester County, New York, HUD authorizes subsidies of $1,552 a month, and in Bergen and Passaic, New Jersey, $1,521; in San Jose, California, $1,507.

* In Pitkin County, Colorado, HUD will pay up to $1,467 a month for a welfare family's housing, and in San Miguel County, Colorado, HUD ups the ante to up to $1,684 a month.

* In Prince George's, Frederick, Calvert, and Charles counties, Maryland, HUD will pay up to $1,396 in rental subsidies per apartment. But, according to local realtors, those counties have few, if any, apartments renting for such high prices.

* Section 8 seeks to end the stigma of being on welfare by treating welfare recipients like self-reliant upper-middle-class citizens. Not surprisingly, with such generous subsidies, many Section 8 recipients enjoy far more comfortable housing than do working

Americans. Pamela Price told the *Los Angeles Times* in March that "this is like Christmas" after she used her new Section 8 certificate to move into a luxurious apartment complex with a heated swimming pool, four spas, six tennis courts, and two air-conditioned racquetball courts. Section 8 certificates are entitling welfare families to move into the Alexander House apartment complex in Silver Spring, Maryland, that boasts a heated pool with water jets, as well as microwave ovens and "deluxe modern kitchens with convenient breakfast bars."

* In May 1994, HUD raised Section 8 subsidy levels in Plano, Texas, to $750 for a two-bedroom and $900 for a three-bedroom apartment. According to HUD, the median rent in Plano, Texas, is only $586 per month. Helen Macey, executive director of the Plano Housing Authority, declared, "Our residents will be given better choices of where they can live." Janice Stanfield, a HUD housing management specialist, explained: "Section 8 is not intended to isolate people or limit them to certain parts of town."

* HUD has vigorously pushed local housing authorities to include mentally ill renters in subsidized housing across the country. Some of the mentally ill renters are violent; one mentally ill renter in Massachusetts won a court victory in summer 1994 on his right to subsidized housing even though he was judged to be a *pyromaniac*.

* Section 8 recipients can pull down a neighborhood because of the paralyzing red tape that HUD imposes on private landlords who want to evict recipients who are troublemakers, hooligans, or deadbeats. A *Boston Globe* editorial complained, "Among the roughly 8,000 families receiving federally subsidized Section 8 rent certificates in Boston, most are concentrated in Roxbury and Dorchester. The majority occupy homes owned by absentee landlords who are reluctant to evict tenants, even for the most egregious lease violations. For landlords, the guaranteed subsidy payment proves a stronger incentive than the desire to maintain a safe building." The *Boston Globe* noted in April 1993 the disrup-

tion caused by Section 8 renters living across the street from Mayor Raymond Flynn: "The subsidized tenants living in the house across the street were nuisances, allegedly using drugs and making loud and threatening noises, but little could be done about it. The landlord had paid no attention. The housing organization that provided the subsidy had thrown up its hands; federal rules forbade it from removing the family from the program."

✳ In Haledon, New Jersey, last fall, a public meeting on Section 8 exploded. As the *Record*, a local newspaper, reported, "The meetings were as rancorous as any ever held in the borough. Residents denounced their neighbors in federally subsidized housing, accusing them of ruining property values and bringing a bad element to the borough. The two meetings held to protest the 'problem' were standing room only."

✳ HUD made starkly clear how it feels welfare recipients should be treated when it financed a luxury housing project in La Jolla, California, a super-rich suburb of San Diego. HUD financed apartments with market values of up to $500,000 each with lavish furnishings and panoramic 180-degree views of the Pacific ocean. HUD selected twenty-eight welfare-recipient families—with incomes as high as $34,000—and gave them the keys to the kind of housing that most Americans can barely dream about. HUD's generosity appalled even some local activists, who recognized that the project would spark great resentment. Mel Shapiro of San Diego told one newspaper: "I'm a housing advocate, but I'm not an idiot."

SUPERFUND:

A Monument to
Bureaucratic Tyranny

Did you send your old car to a junkyard after it reached its 200,000-mile limit? Then federal agents could arrive at your door and hit you with a $10 million cleanup bill, demanding that you pay for the cleanup of the entire junkyard.

The Superfund program, enacted by Congress in 1980, was supposed to solve the problems of abandoned hazardous-waste sites across the American landscape. Unfortunately, Superfund is now largely "an expensive dump site beautification exercise."

Tens of billions of dollars have been spent by the federal government, corporations, individuals, and even churches to pay for the cleanup of waste sites. Yet, the EPA has screwed up the program so badly that Superfund has now long since qualified for the U.S. Government Boondoggle Hall of Fame.

In EPA's interpretation of the law, EPA claims it has a right to impose the entire cost of cleaning up a hazardous-waste site on any company, individual, or organization who contributed a single box of garbage or trash to that site. Even when the EPA has no reliable evidence that a company actually sent waste products to a Superfund site, it does not hesitate to file multimillion-dollar lawsuits against the company to bankroll its inefficient cleanup efforts.

Superfund is a retroactive law par excellence. Even though a company or individual may have obeyed all the laws existing at the time when it sent its waste products to a dump, the company can still be forced to pay the entire cost of the dump's cleanup.

EPA has effectively no burden to prove that a company sent waste to a Superfund site; instead, the company must prove itself innocent of ever having sent anything to a site. As one lawyer observed, "It is as if the EPA is asking your client, 'When did you stop sending hazardous waste to the site?' "

* At the Ludlow Sanitary Landfill in New York, hundreds of businesses and nonprofit organizations have been forced to pay massive cleanup costs, including a hospital, several public schools, and a pizza parlor.

* While most Americans think of dangerous hazardous-waste sites as being the fault of highly polluting industries, the EPA listed a pet cemetery owner as one of the responsible parties for Superfund cleanup costs at a Tulsa, Oklahoma, site.

* A small camera and film-developing store was held liable for the massive cleanup costs of a Superfund site in Glenwood Landing, New York.

* Hundreds of businesses were held liable for the cleanup costs of the Lorentz Barrel and Drum Superfund site in San Jose, California—even though the California Department of the Environment required the companies to send their empty oil drums to a recycler, and the Lorentz site was the only one in the state.

* EPA was spending, during the late 1980s, over $7 on overhead for each $1 that it spent on Superfund cleanups.

* A study by the Congressional Office of Technology Assessment concluded that half of all Superfund cleanups "address hypothetical risks rather than actual ones."

* The OTA also concluded that up to two-thirds of all Superfund spending is "inefficient and undermines the environmental mission of the program."

* State and local governments are forcing companies to pay for cleaning up government landfills. This happens even in cases in which city employees are blatantly responsible for problems at the landfills. Attorney George Freeman told the Senate Judiciary Committee, "The city of New York has brought a Superfund suit to clean up its landfill, even though the illicit disposal resulted from one of its own employees dealing with organized crime."

* Former Interior Department chief economist Richard Stroup observed, "At one site EPA went to court and required parties to spend 9.3 million additional dollars to clean the site to a level where the dirt would be safe enough to eat for 260 days a year. EPA was unsatisfied with 'contaminated' dirt that everyone conceded was safe to eat for 70 days a year. And the site was in a swamp!"

* At the Nyzanda chemical waste Superfund site in Ashland, Massachusetts, EPA has spent $25 million—and plans to spend hundreds of millions more. As *Forbes* reported, "Superfund staffers acknowledge that the site's risk to human health is now negligible. But the rules say: Keep cleaning anyhow. Superfund staffers also acknowledge that the 20-odd people mugged to pay the tab, local small landowners and entrepreneurs, never actually contributed to the pollution."

* Kent Jeffreys of the National Center for Policy Analysis has observed, "The main problem is that Superfund is lying to people. No one has had the courage to say if you drink coffee every morning, under the standards of Superfund, you are receiving ten thousand times the exposure rate." The stricter the cleanup standards the EPA imposes, the more power agency officials have over private companies—since companies will have to spend far more to meet EPA's stringent standards.

* EPA exercises extreme power over potentially responsible parties. It effectively compels the parties to sign "consent decrees" accepting responsibility for the cost of cleanups—yet the EPA reserves the right to abrogate the consent decrees unilaterally at its own convenience at any time.

* EPA compels companies to accept liability for a waste-site cleanup by threats of triple damages for EPA-funded cleanup costs, as well as fines of $25,000 a day. After the EPA labeled the soil under a pesticide factory near Cape Giradeau, Missouri, as a Superfund site, EPA reached a settlement with the family that owned the company; the company agreed to repay the estimated $2 million cleanup cost. As part of the settlement, EPA and the company agreed that the factory would be decontaminated but not destroyed, as a *Wall Street Journal* editorial noted. In early 1993, EPA nullified the agreement and announced plans to destroy the factory building (the agency claimed that would save money). EPA justified its decision to destroy the building by claiming that it could not afford to analyze the tests it made of the building "due to budget constraints." When the building owners protested, EPA informed them that the agency had nothing to discuss with them. Federal judge Stephen Limbaugh intervened: "It is clear to the court that the EPA's 'concern about public safety and the increasing costs to taxpayers' is insincere and sanctimonious. The EPA's refusal to communicate with the defendants about the demolition of their building, and its arrogant pontificating, reflect nothing less than an attitude of supremacy tantamount to contempt." The judge concluded that EPA's cleanup goals do "not make it an administrative deity" and that Congress "did not intend to give the EPA unfettered authority to deceive and bully people into submission."

* In February 1995, EPA chief Carol Browner announced that the federal government intended to remove twenty-five thousand properties from its list of potential Superfund sites across the country. (Roughly thirteen thousand sites will remain on the list.) Browner conceded that even after a Superfund site is re-

moved from a neighborhood, the area "loses jobs, loses its tax base, loses hope. . . . It was never intended that the Superfund program would make that problem worse." Browner's statement is effectively an admission of EPA's gross failure—a confession that a government cleanup program may have disrupted far more lives than the hazardous wastes themselves.

The Typhoid Mary Full Employment Act

Federal civil rights policy is threatening public health and making it more likely that Americans will be exposed to contagious fatal diseases.

In 1987, the Supreme Court, in a pathbreaking decision, ruled that a school board wrongfully fired a teacher with tuberculosis. TB is highly contagious and can be spread simply by molecules passed in the air. The Supreme Court proclaimed, "It would be unfair to allow an employer to seize upon the distinction between the effects of a [contagious] disease on others and the effects of a disease on a patient and use that distinction to justify discriminatory treatment."

With that one sweeping sentence, people with contagious diseases were put in the same "protected group" that the civil rights law had carved out for blacks, Hispanics, and other groups perceived to be victims of widespread prejudice.

The Americans with Disabilities Act of 1990 further slanted public policy against public safety. Under current federal regulations, "any physiological disorder or condition" can be classified as a handicap which employers are prohibited from discriminating on the basis of. Since contagious diseases are physiological disorders, voilà!—discriminating against people with contagious disease becomes a federal crime.

Employers are now required to hire people with contagious diseases unless they can prove that the person poses a large risk to other
workers or their customers.

✳ It is extremely unlikely that someone could contract AIDS as a
result of eating a meal prepared by an AIDS-infected person.
However, the federal Centers for Disease Control in 1993 revised
the definition of AIDS to include people who are HIV-positive
and have developed tuberculosis or recurrent pneumonia. Both
TB and pneumonia are highly contagious. A Farmington, Connecticut, restaurant was sued by the state Commission on Human
Rights and Opportunities after the restaurant refused to rehire an
HIV-positive waiter who had taken a leave after coming down
with double pneumonia. (The *Hartford Courant* noted that the
waiter "started losing weight and became sluggish and weak. He
left his food under the warmers too long, and his hands shook so
much that he couldn't carry cocktail trays.")

✳ Federal judge Joyce Hens Green ruled in 1993 that the D.C. fire
department violated an infectious firefighter's civil rights because
he was specifically prohibited from doing mouth-to-mouth resuscitation. But the firefighter had hepatitis B (one hundred times
more contagious than AIDS), which infects three hundred thousand people and kills seven thousand people a year.

✳ The biggest impact of the new discrimination-contagion policy is
on health care. The ADA's mandate could produce deadly results
from the thousands of HIV-positive physicians in this country. A
1992 federal Centers for Disease Control study observed that "the
estimated probability that [an HIV-infected] surgeon will transmit HIV at least once during the rest of his/her career is 8.1
percent."

✳ Even if a surgeon with HIV lies to his patients and claims not to
be infected, the surgeon is still entitled to full protection under
the disabilities act. Dr. Philip Benson, a Minneapolis physician,
continued delivering babies and doing invasive genital and rectal

examinations for nearly a year after he came down with AIDS. The Minnesota Board of Medical Examiners in September 1990 permitted him to continue practicing even after he had open sores on his hands and arms as long as he wore double gloves. Benson reportedly lied to his patients when they asked questions about his sores and his sharp weight loss (he claimed he was on a "crash diet"), and also failed to wear gloves during some examinations. Under the ADA, an AIDS-infected physician can lie to his patients about his own health—yet it can be a federal crime for a hospital to honestly disclose the infected condition of one of its doctors.

✳ While many HIV-infected surgeons voluntarily cease practicing, others are not so inclined. In late 1992, an AIDS-infected orthopedic surgeon sued Mercy Catholic Medical Center of Philadelphia for revoking his hospital privileges. The hospital offered to allow the surgeon to continue practicing if his patients signed consent forms stating that they had been informed of the doctor's HIV status.

The surgeon considered this a violation of his rights and sued, demanding compensatory damages and restoration of surgical privileges. The doctor's lawyers declared that he was bringing "this action to vindicate his right, and the rights of other qualified people with disabilities, to fair treatment and equal opportunity." *American Medical News* noted, "Advocates for people with HIV insist that requiring notification [of patients] is tantamount to revoking [hospital] privileges." A federal judge upheld the hospital's action, ruling that the hospital "reasonably decided that Dr. Paul Scoles's patients should not undergo an invasive procedure without knowledge of his HIV status." Attorney Catherine Hanssens, who represented Scoles, denounced the ruling, claiming that the court indicated that "it's okay to effectively destroy his career."

✳ The failure of policies that indulge infectious surgeons was made stark in a recent investigation of a UCLA surgeon who spread hepatitis B to eighteen patients undergoing heart surgery in 1991 and 1992. Amazingly, the hospital had tested the surgeon, discovered he was infected, and yet still allowed him to continue operating on patients without warning patients of the additional deadly risks they faced. The hepatitis was apparently spread to patients through tiny holes in surgical gloves. The *New York Times* noted in 1994 that "the hospital's decision to allow the surgeon to keep on operating even after he was found to be infected . . . is in compliance with Federal guidelines."

VITAMINS:

The Federal War
on Dietary Supplements

Should federal bureaucrats have unlimited power over the type of vitamins that American citizens can take?

FDA agents have carried out scores of armed raids against the stores and homes of vitamin and dietary supplement producers and sellers.

* In 1990, armed FDA agents and federal marshals raided the home of Kim Scott in Mount Angel, Oregon. She and her father had been mailing reprints of an article from *Omni* magazine along with their bottles of coenzyme Q10, a supplement believed by many to boost heart performance. The FDA claimed that since the *Omni* article made health claims about the supplement which the FDA did not approve, the agency had a right to confiscate the drug.

* On May 6, 1992, a platoon of sixteen FDA inspectors and heavily armed local police in flak jackets carried out a no-knock raid, smashing in the door of the Tahoma Health clinic in Kent, Washington, and held the staff at gunpoint in case anybody would try to hide the vitamins. The raiders seized over $100,000 worth of products and office supplies (including address books and diaries); they spent fourteen hours cleaning out the office, and even tore

phones out of the wall. FDA agents were especially concerned about the clinic's use of injectable B vitamins, a product which has been widely used in Germany with no adverse health problems. Though the FDA claimed that Dr. Jonathan Wright—a highly visible critic of the agency and the clinic's owner—was engaged in dangerous health practices, it has not filed any charges against him in court. And, more than three years after the seizure, the FDA has refused to return any of the office records or other material it seized.

* An agency created to safeguard Americans from deadly perils is instead increasingly spending its time worrying about such things as innocuous claims made about dog biscuits. On January 13, 1994, the Northeast Region of the FDA threatened Jane Morrill, publisher of a supplements catalog, because of comments she wrote about a dog biscuit containing yeast and garlic bits which would help keep fleas away from pets. FDA official Edward J. McDonnell sent her a warning letter, informing her that the claims in her catalog "are drug claims which cause the product to be a new animal drug without an approved New Animal Drug Application. Such product, is unsafe within the meaning of Section 512 of the Federal Food Drug and Cosmetic Act, and adulterated for purposes of section 501 (a) (5)." The FDA threatened seizures and injunctions unless the woman ceased making any claims for her dog biscuits. Since Morrill did not have a million or two dollars in spare change to pass through the FDA approval gauntlet, she muzzled herself.

* Others who did not bow to the FDA's demands are not so lucky: in 1990, Sissy McGill, owner of Solid Gold Pet Foods in El Cajon, California, was jailed for 179 days and fined $10,000 after the FDA prosecuted her for claiming that her dog food offered pooches "a longer and healthier life."

* Over one hundred million Americans currently take dietary supplements to bolster diets, enhance well-being, or combat illness. In 1992, the FDA proposed regulations that would have effec-

tively prohibited the sale of most medicinal herbs and effectively slashed the dosage of vitamins. The health food lobby rallied and beat back the FDA. But in late 1993, the FDA issued regulations that prevent almost all vitamin makers from claiming any health benefits from their products. At the same time, the consensus in the scientific community—based on hundreds of articles in medical journals—on the benefits of vitamins has become stronger than ever.

* In 1992, the U.S. Public Health Service concluded that the consumption of 400 micrograms of folic acid (a B vitamin) a day by expectant mothers could reduce the number of neural tube defects, such as spina bifida, among newborn babies by 50 percent. Between two and three thousand babies are born with spina bifida every year. The FDA, however, threatened criminal prosecution against any vitamin maker that advertised the health benefits of folic acid for pregnant women. As attorney Jonathan Emord notes, "The FDA has even denounced the National Institutes of Health for making 'false and misleading' statements about the health benefits of folic acid."

The FDA finally succumbed to the overwhelming weight of scientific evidence and agreed in late 1993 that vitamin makers could mention that folic acid may reduce birth defects—but continues to refuse to allow them to mention that the defects may be reduced by 50 percent.

* The FDA has repeatedly sought control over nutrition supplements by claiming that they are actually food additives—and thus that the producers must prove to the FDA that the supplements are safe. (According to one study, it can cost up to $2 million and require up to six years for the FDA to approve a petition for a new food additive.)

WETLANDS:

Locking Up Landowners
for the Birds

If a migrating bird sees a wet spot on your property, federal agents can prohibit you from using your land. A single flock of "glancing geese" can turn a person's life savings into a compulsory bird sanctuary. And if you refuse to submit to federal agents' bird-serving demands, then you could be going up the river for a stay in federal prison. Even though Congress never placed wetlands under the control of federal bureaucrats, the bureaucrats have been waging a vendetta against private landowners.

★ At a House Judiciary Committee hearing in February 1995, Nancy Cline, a mother of five young children in Sonoma, California, testified about how federal bureaucrats had practically destroyed her and her husband's lives. Her husband bought 350 acres of farmland in Sonoma to establish a winery. Even though the land had been farmed for over sixty years, an Army Corps of Engineers agent came and told him to stop farming it because it was a wetland. Although Cline agreed to stop plowing, the agent claimed to have "discovered an unauthorized activity" taking place on the farm and issued a cease and desist order with penalties of $25,000 per day and imprisonment of up to one year if Cline continued farming.

Congress clearly specified that normal farm operations would be exempt from the wetlands designation under the Clean Water Act. The Army Corps chose to ignore the congressional directive in its pursuit of the Clines. The Clines repeatedly requested meetings with Army Corps officials to discuss and resolve their issue, but the federal agents never had time to discuss the matter with them.

Ms. Cline testified, "In November 1992, a letter arrived from the corps. Despite the massive and expensive documentation provided by our attorney, we were told we had forty-five days to . . . fill in any agricultural ditches, restore the site to its pre-agricultural state, post a bond for the corps to be assured of our intentions, and be prepared to hire an environmental consultant for five years to monitor the site according to the corps's wishes."

When the Clines refused to bow to the Army Corps' demands, the feds upped the ante and launched a criminal investigation. As Cline related,

> In January 1994, the FBI showed up. Obviously the Corps had no desire to discuss or resolve this issue. We were told to hire a criminal attorney. . . . Their issue was power and control. Their issue was an edict from the U.S. Attorney General demanding more criminal environmental convictions in the Ninth Circuit apparently short of the prescribed quotas.
>
> The FBI and EPA interrogated neighbors, acquaintances and strangers. They asked about our religion, whether we were intelligent, did we have tempers. They asked how we treat our children.
>
> Our property was surveyed by military blackhawk helicopters. Their cars monitored our home and our children's school. They accused Fred of paying neighbors to lie. The FBI actually told one terrified neighbor that this investigation was top secret, with national security implications. The community reeled, as did we.
>
> Our personal papers were subpoenaed. The grand jury was convened.
>
> We spent thousands of additional dollars to hire more attor-

neys. The Justice Department told our attorneys that—unless we would plead guilty and surrender our land they would seek a criminal indictment of both Fred and me. According to one government attorney, I was to be included because I had written a letter to the editor of the local paper in their opinion, "publicly undermining the authority of the Army Corps."

In December 1994, the Justice Department informed the Clines' attorney that the government had chosen not to proceed on criminal charges. Yet the Army Corps has refused to resolve the issue.

Cline told the congressional committee that she knew she risked retaliation by speaking up, but felt that she had to do it. She said that she and her husband had spent over $100,000 thus far, to fight the government for the right to use their own land. She bitterly complained of the federal agents: "They had no right to strip Fred and me of our dreams. They had no right to force us to spend our children's legacy to protect ourselves from incarceration, from prison. This is not about protecting the environment. It's about agencies out of control and in need of adult supervision. . . . These agents have stolen our dreams and our land. If they want our land, I urge you to make them pay for it."

★ Grace Heck, a seventy-seven-year-old woman from Farmingdale, New Jersey, also submitted testimony to the House Judiciary Committee for its February 1995 hearing on wetlands abuses. Mrs. Heck was not allowed to testify after the subcommittee chairman Charles Canady got nervous after receiving a call from a journalist making unsubstantiated accusations against Mrs. Heck and her husband. As *Washington Times* editorial writer Ken Smith later showed, the charges were part of a smear campaign carefully orchestrated by environmental groups to try to destroy the credibility of people complaining about federal violations of their property rights.

Mrs. Heck related how she and her eighty-two-year-old husband—who had had eight heart attacks—had been devastated by the Army Corps of Engineers. The Hecks had twenty-five acres of land, which a local government had approved for building a forty-five-house subdivision. But, after the Army Corps expanded the definition of wetlands in 1987, the project was blocked. The Army Corps claimed that the hardwood forest was actually a wetland. Additionally, the U.S. Fish and Wildlife Service protested that the project should not be approved because a federally threatened plant species was "within five miles of the proposed project site."

The land was practically the only asset that the Hecks possessed; after the Army Corps's ruling, it became practically worthless. Instead of selling their property for $2 million, the Hecks were driven into near destitution—forced to move into their daughter's small house, no longer able to afford their family doctor, not even able to afford hearing aids. Mrs. Heck bitterly complained: "We have never asked our government for anything. We were proud to be Americans. Now we are ashamed of our country and a government that allows the bureaucrats to steal from its citizens under the false pretense that it is for the public good."

✦ Gaston and Monique Roberge bought several acres of undeveloped land in Orchard Beach, Maine, in 1964. In 1976, they allowed the city government to dump some clean fill onto part of their lot. In 1986, a developer offered the couple $440,000 for their land—which the two of them consider their personal "retirement fund." But the Army Corps of Engineers announced that the land had miraculously become a wetland—largely because the Roberges had allowed the local government to place the clean dirt on the land. After Gaston Roberge publicly complained about what he considered an unfair decision, Army Corps field officer Jay Clement wrote a memo to his superiors stating, "Roberge would be a good one to squash and set an example." The Roberges fought the feds in court, and the government paid the couple over $300,000 last year to settle their lawsuit alleging that the U.S. had "effectively and unjustifiably grabbed the property."

✦ Ocie Mills, a Florida builder, and his son were sent to prison for two years for placing clean sand on a quarter-acre lot he owned. Mills had been a vocal critic of the EPA in Navarre, Florida—so he was targeted for punishment by prosecutors and bureaucrats. As the Washington Legal Foundation noted, "The EPA did not file any civil enforcement action and instead sought criminal indictments. If EPA's goal was truly environmental protection, EPA would have filed a civil suit ordering the removal of the so-called 'pollutant.' Instead, the sand remained on the property over two years while Mr. Mills and his son were in prison." After Mills was released from the pen, he filed suit to have his felony conviction overturned. Federal Judge Roger Vinson, ruling on Mills's suit in 1993, denounced the federal government's wetlands interpretations as a "regulatory hydra . . . worthy of *Alice in Wonderland*." Judge Vinson concluded: "A jurisprudence which allows Congress to impliedly delegate its criminal lawmaking authority to a regulatory agency such as the Army Corps—so long as the Congress provides an 'intelligible principle' to guide that agency—is enough to make any judge pause and question what has happened." Judge Vinson denounced a bureaucratic interpretation according to which "a landowner who places clean fill dirt on a plot of subdivided dry *land* may be imprisoned for the statutory felony offense of discharging pollutants into the navigable *waters* of the United States."

★ Pennsylvania resident John Pocysgai was sent to prison for two years for putting several truckloads of dirt on a malarial section of a junkyard that he had cleaned up. The government claimed that the junkyard was a wetland.

★ Louise and Frederic Williams saw their Little Compton, Rhode Island, property plummet in value by almost 90 percent—from $260,000 to less than $30,000—after federal agents declared the land wetlands. The Williamses, who in 1988 had started construction on a new home on the five-acre plot, were ordered by state environmental officials to tear down the partly built structure, and, at their own expense, follow a precise thirteen-point property restoration plan. Mrs. Williams complained: "Not only did we have to plant what they dictated, but we had to make sure the trees were alive and well when they inspected them the next year."

* Wetlands rulings have had devastating impacts on thousands of property owners. The Congressional Budget Office estimates that it would cost at least $10 billion to compensate owners for the loss of their property values as a result of wetlands rulings.

* In 1985, one EPA lawyer wrote a memo to other EPA lawyers, unilaterally greatly extending the agency's power under the Clean Water Act. After the memo was circulated among EPA offices, the agency began a new and startling power grab: claiming that federal wetlands authority extends to any patch of moist land that a migrating bird happens to glance at while flying over—the now-infamous "glancing geese" test. Hoffman Homes, Inc., a Chicago-area builder, was hit by a $50,000 penalty by the EPA for the crime of placing dirt on a small moist corner of a development. Hoffman sued the EPA, claiming that the agency's "glancing geese" rule had no basis in federal law. Federal judge Daniel Manion rebuked the agency in 1992: "The EPA claims jurisdiction . . . solely on the ground that migratory birds could, potentially, use the wetland as a place to feed or nest or as a stopover on the way to the Gulf states for the winter months." Manion observed, "In fact, there is not even any evidence that migratory birds, or any other wildlife, actually used the area for any purpose. . . . After April showers not every temporary wet spot necessarily becomes subject to government control." (Manion's sagacious decision was overturned by other federal judges.)

* Even the smallest amount of alleged wetland can be sufficient to allow federal bureaucrats to seize control and paralyze owners. John Piazza, president of a construction company, received a permit from his local government to build a ministorage facility on a seven-acre tract in Mount Vernon, Washington. But a federal agent found three small alleged wet areas on the land. Piazza redesigned his facility so that it would affect only .18 acre of wetland. He resubmitted his proposal to the Army Corps of Engineers and waited, waited, and waited. While Piazza's revised application was gathering dust, the federal government redefined wetlands—and, under the new definition, the ministorage project should have affected only .089 acre of wetland. Federal enforcers

announced that Piazza would have to contribute $25,000 to a federal fund to buy wetlands elsewhere before he could build, as environmental analyst Jonathan Tolman reported in the *Wall Street Journal*.

* The Army Corps and the EPA are imposing their controls over sections of a development as small as twenty-six square feet— roughly half the size of a Ping-Pong table. One Rhode Island town was forced to wait for almost two years to get federal permission to do mosquito control work on .009 acre of wetland. When federal bureaucrats assert control over such a tiny square in a plot of land, they can effectively prohibit the owner from building on a much greater portion of his property. The legal costs of getting government permission to build on or near a suspected wetland can easily exceed $50,000—a prohibitive cost for most individual land owners.

ZONING:

The New American Dictatorship

Local zoning officials are ruling and ruining the lives of average citizens. Modern zoning laws presume that no citizen has a right to control his own land—and that every citizen has a right to control his neighbor's land. Zoning laws have become far more invasive and restrictive in recent years.

* Columbia, Maryland, requires new homes to have sprinkler systems installed in the lawn—which adds hundreds of dollars to the price of building a new house.

* Zoning officials are in the front line of this nation's war against pumpkin abuse. In December 1993, the village of East Hampton, Long Island, issued a warrant for the arrest of a food shop owner guilty of an unauthorized exhibition of large orange gourds, as the *New York Times* reported. Jerry Della Femina, the co-owner of Jerry and David's Red Horse Market, had a few dozen pumpkins stacked in front of his store. Village bureaucrats ruled that the pumpkins were the equivalent of a sign advertising the sale of pumpkins, and thus the owner needed a sign permit. (The shop was in a historic district, and government officials may have thought that similar markets in East Hampton in the nineteenth century never placed pumpkins in front of their stores.) Larry

Cantwell, the village administrator, explained, "The village takes its code seriously and feels it has no alternative but to enforce it."

* Design police are also driving people to distraction in Del Mar, California, a suburb of San Diego. One Del Mar resident, Brian Sesco, was forced to change his house design nine times; the delays caused him to lose the property due to bank foreclosure, as the *San Diego Tribune* reported in 1993. Sesco stated that his marriage failed because of the stress of the battle with the design review board. One family complained that it took them two and a half years to get their home built—and they had to spend an extra $50,000 on changes to meet the board's demands. Local architect Lou Dominy observed: "My guess is that some of the board members can't even read architectural plans. But here they are wasting people's time and money and sitting up there making subjective views on design that they can't even understand." City government planning official Adam Birnbaum justified the process as "a long one because it is meant to involve a great deal of public participation. The idea behind it is that everyone can give their ideas to the board as to what they think is appropriate design." But why should everyone be allowed to stick his thumb into the design of other people's property?

* Coral Gables, Florida, charges residents thirty-five dollars to get a permit to paint the bathroom in their home—or the living room, or any other room. Local building inspectors patrol the streets looking for painting trucks parked at homes that have not paid the permit fee.

* Stephen Page, a corporate executive, was dragged through a five-year hell by Pacific Grove, California. Page wanted to buy and build a home on a one acre plot on Sunset Drive in Pacific Grove, California. The city government requested that Page wait a year before closing on the land so that the city itself could try to raise the money to buy it and leave it undeveloped. Page honored the request, but the city failed to raise its money. Page related in the *Wall Street Journal*:

In order to get a building permit, we were required to seek the approval of three layers of government: The Architectural Review Board, the planning Commission, and finally, the City Council. . . . Over a two year period, we endured 20 public hearings regarding the size, shape, height, siting, texture, materials and color of our proposed residence. During one of 11 public Architectural Review Board meetings, an ARB commissioner opined: "In my former life as a seagull, I was flying up and down the California coastline and saw your house built shaped as a seashell, rather like a Nautilus seashell, built out of driftwood and feathers, with the aperture facing out to sea."

Page eventually won permission to build his house after suing the city government—and after spending $600,000 for carrying costs, lawyers, and environmental impact statement, as well as geological and botanical surveys for the site.

* Anti-monotony decrees are a new favorite of zoners. "Carol Stream, Illinois, has a seven-page ordinance spelling out what makes a house dissimilar: from height and styles of roof line to the shape and number of windows to types of building materials. And don't try painting even a few shades of blue away from your neighbor's facades. Only an entirely different color will be allowed," as the *Chicago Tribune* reported.

* New Lenox, Illinois, passed an ordinance in 1993 declaring that it would not issue a building permit for "any single family detached dwelling unit which is similar in appearance to any dwelling on the same street which is within two lots distance to it."

* Tinley Park, Illinois, decreed that "no two single-family dwellings of identical . . . facade" can be next to one another, and identical houses cannot make up more than 25 percent of all the houses on a block. Tinley Park building commissioner Ray Fessler explained: "It wouldn't be fair if you bought this house and had it built and all of a sudden the next customer built the same one next door." But this concept of fairness is simply a charade for bureaucrats to justify awarding themselves more power.

✶ The *Arizona Republic* reported in 1994 that Gilbert, Arizona, planning director Scot Anderson had plans for Gilbert to be the first municipality southeast of Phoenix "to force variety in new housing." This is ironic, since the clearest, most consistent impact of government regulation is to impose uniformity. (Many developers have complained that rigid zoning codes across the country have prevented them from including more variations in new subdivisions.) After government regulations impose uniformity, bureaucrats decide the answer is not to decrease regulations, but to create new regulations to "force variety."

✶ In September 1993, the New York City buildings commissioner bushwhacked Fordham University. Fordham had received permission from the city government to build a 480-foot radio tower at its campus in the Bronx. After the radio tower was almost half finished, the city government reversed its position and revoked the building permit. The government's action cost Fordham over half a million dollars.

✶ In a 1991 ruling, a federal appeals court ruled that the Puerto Rico government, in revoking, delaying, and denying permission for an already approved resort to be built by the PFZ Corporation, "violated state law," "failed to comply with the agency regulations or practices," "arbitrarily or capriciously refused to process [PFZ's] approved construction drawings," "engaged in delaying tactics and refused to issue permits . . . based on considerations outside the scope of its jurisdiction," and that these unlawful acts "injured [PFZ's] property." Yet the court refused to rule against the Puerto Rican government, concluding that "bad-faith permit denials or arbitrary refusals" to follow state law "simply do not amount to a deprivation of due process." The court announced that, for a zoning action to be a violation of a property owner's rights, the government's action would have to be an "abuse of government power that shocks the conscience." Since the judges' consciences were not shocked by the government's abuse of PFZ, the corporation was out of luck.